YORKSHIRE'S SEASIDE PIERS

YORKSHIRE'S SEASIDE PIERS

Martin Easdown

Wharncliffe Books

First published in Great Britain in 2008 by
Wharncliffe Books
An imprint of
Pen & Sword Books Ltd
47 Church Street
Barnsley
South Yorkshire
S70 2AS

Copyright © Martin Easdown 2008

ISBN 978 1 84563 062 1

A CIP catalogue record for this book is
available from the British Library

Typeset by Mac Style, Nafferton, East Yorkshire
Printed and bound in the UK by CPI

Pen & Sword Books Ltd incorporates the Imprints of Pen & Sword
Aviation, Pen & Sword Maritime, Pen & Sword Military,
Wharncliffe Local History, Pen & Sword Select,
Pen & Sword Military Classics, Leo Cooper, Remember When,
Seaforth Publishing and Frontline Publishing

For a complete list of Pen & Sword titles please contact
PEN & SWORD BOOKS LIMITED
47 Church Street, Barnsley, South Yorkshire, S70 2AS, England
E-mail: enquiries@pen-and-sword.co.uk
Website: www.pen-and-sword.co.uk

CONTENTS

PREFACE

There is something enchanting about piers, something doubtless connected with the fact that they create a world of their own halfway between land and sea.

Keith Turner
Pier Railways

A s Archivist of the National Piers Society, I have long been fascinated with Yorkshire's long-lost seaside pleasure piers; ever since I 'discovered' piers in 1987 through the book *Seaside Piers* by Simon Adamson. My architectural eye caught the graceful beauty of Redcar Pier's ironwork, whilst my historical eye wondered why Scarborough, Hornsea, Withernsea and Coatham had lost their piers so long ago.

I became fascinated by piers and their history. The pleasure pier is one of the most evocative symbols of the British seaside, and as a maritime nation it is not surprising that the pier (with its wooden deck like a ship and naval-attired pier masters) became such a popular feature of our coast.

My first written account of Yorkshire's pleasure piers, *Piers of Disaster* in 1996, was largely unsatisfactory due to the text being compiled from secondary sources, which have proved not always to be reliable. Thanks to Wharncliffe Books I am now able to retell their story in a fuller, more accurate account utilising the many new illustrations that I have acquired in the intervening twelve years.

I have endeavoured to fully research the history of each of the six piers, using newspapers, guides, books and archive material held at record offices. Having been conceived, born, and in some cases died, during the Victorian period, this book unashamedly concentrates on the story of the piers during this period. The subsequent histories of the two piers that survived beyond the early years of the twentieth century, Saltburn and Redcar, are covered but not in the same detail. Ironically, early source material on the one surviving pier, Saltburn, is less in abundance than its long-lost cousins.

Yorkshire's Seaside Piers strictly covers only the six seaside pleasure piers that were constructed on the county's coastline. A pleasure pier is usually defined as a purpose-built cast iron or steel structure providing use as a promenade and landing stage. Some kind of amusement had to be provided and a toll charged for promenading. Therefore, the harbour and landing piers at Bridlington, Whitby and Hull are covered only briefly in the introductory chapter, although they were popular as promenades in their own right. Also briefly covered are the proposed pleasure piers at Bridlington and Filey.

With a truncated Saltburn the only survivor of Yorkshire's six pleasure piers, I hope this book serves as a suitable memorial to those that were lost long ago in the mists of time.

Martin Easdown
2008

CHAPTER ONE

A STROLL INTO THE NORTH SEA

THE YORKSHIRE SEASIDE TOWNS AND THEIR PIERS

Before the popularisation of the seaside resort from the mid-eighteenth century, most British people regarded the sea with some suspicion and danger. Agreed, it acted as a defence barrier for the island and it provided food, yet it was also dangerous and unpredictable and a graveyard for the nation's seafarers and fishermen. Coastal villages tended to turn their backs on the sea, and the beach was no more than just a gathering place for food and the means of getting into a boat.

Notwithstanding, Yorkshire's principal seaside resort, Scarborough, had been popular with visitors since 1626 when Elizabeth Farrier discovered the underground spring that led to the establishment of the Spa. This was at a time of a re-emergence of the Roman practice of bathing in and drinking mineral-rich waters at spas.

The curative properties of the spring led to the landed gentry of the north to partake of the waters, which were further advertised by Dr Robert Wittie's *Scarborough Spaw, or A Description of the Nature and Vertues of the Spaw at Scarborough in Yorkshire* (1660). In addition to his claim that the spa water could cure every known ailment under the sun, Wittie (in the second edition of the book published in 1667) recommended bathing in the sea for gout sufferers. Scarborough's unique stance as the only major spa to be located by the sea thus led it also to become Britain's first seaside resort. By 1733 the world's first bathing machines were in use and in 1787 there were twenty-six operating in the South Bay. However, they did not come cheap: bathers paid as much as a shilling for a machine and horse, and another shilling for the dippers, two each for the ladies (who wore flannels) and one for the gents (who bathed nude). In addition, Scarborough's wealthy visitors had to pay for subscription to the Spa. In 1733 this was 5s for men and 2s for ladies, with the waters a further shilling an anker. Donner's Long Room, established in the 1720s, cost a further 5s (later increased to 1guinea) subscription to partake of its balls, dances, dress nights and card and billiard tables. Entrance to the coffee house was an additional 2s 6d subscription. The peak number of subscribers to the Spa was 766 in 1748 (who each paid 7s 6d) but thereafter patronage declined in favour of sea bathing and other attractions that were established in the town. In addition to Donner's Long Room, they included Newstead's Long Room (1736), Sandside Long Room (c.1750), Theatre Royal (1767) and a number of circulating libraries.

By 1800, the drinking of seawater in Scarborough (as championed by Dr Richard Russell at Brighton in the 1750s) was more popular than the partaking of the spa water. The fashion for bathing in seawater was also made more comfortable with the opening of indoor baths, including Travis's (1798), McBean's (1800), Weddell's (1812) and Vickerman's (1829).

Access to the Spa was improved from 19 July 1827 with the opening of the Cliff (or Spa) Bridge by the Scarborough Cliff Bridge Company. However a toll of 6d was set by the company to use the bridge and spa. Two years later the Rotunda Museum was erected close to the bridge by the Scarborough Philosophical Society. Designed in the Roman Doric style, the building was circular in order to show off a geological stratification of the Yorkshire Coast. Two side wings were later added to the building in 1861.

The 1820s also saw the development of elegant bow-fronted terraces, including York Place, Brunswick Terrace, Vernon Place and Falsgrave Walk, followed by The Crescent and Belvoir Terrace in the 1830s. Purpose-built hotels such as the Crown (1844) and the Queens (1848) were erected from the 1840s, culminating in Cuthbert Broderick's breathtaking Grand Hotel (1867). This was the largest hotel in Europe at the time and the prototype for all the following 'Grand' seaside hotels (although they could never match it). The hotel took four years to build and cost £100,000, which led to the bankruptcy of the promoting company. The building boasted four domes (representing the seasons), twelve floors (months), fifty-two chimneys (weeks) and 365 rooms (days). In 1870 the Pavilion Hotel was opened close to the railway station, the first train from York having arrived on 7 July 1845. The 'Queen of Watering Places' was flourishing and also gained new Assembly Rooms (1851), Joseph Paxton's Grand Hall at the Spa (1858) and modern seawater baths on the South Sands (1859). The railway was also bringing in increasing numbers of the wealthier middle-class visitor, who favoured the Alexandra Music Hall (1858) and the Globe and Pantheon Theatres (1860s).

Industrialisation during the nineteenth century proceeded rapidly and the population concentrated in the large cities and industrial areas. Paid holidays were an exception, although unpaid days off (particularly Mondays after weekend pay days) were common. Christmas Day and Good Friday were the only recognised bank holidays: the amount of holidays having actually been cut during the Industrial Revolution. The Factory Act of 1833 stipulated that persons under eighteen should be entitled to eight half day holidays per year alongside Christmas Day, Good Friday, and because it became impracticable to apply the law to only part of the workforce, it was often applied to all. Some bosses however took advantage of loopholes in the law not to apply it and many thought their workers abused their leisure time by drinking too much. Some factories took time off for local wakes fairs and Whitsuntide, and also occasionally Easter Monday and New Years Day but it was not until the passing of the Bank Holiday Act in 1871 that Whit Monday, Boxing Day, Easter Monday and the first Monday in August would join Christmas Day and Good Friday as paid holidays. By the final quarter of the nineteenth century many middle class and some working class people were earning enough money for a week's paid holiday to enjoy the curative sea air away from the grimy smoky towns. The money had often been saved by paying into a savings club at a factory where they worked. Each different Lancashire and Yorkshire industrial town staggered their annual wakes week holiday, although the Lancashire coast (and principally Blackpool and Morecambe) was the favoured destination for these. The main clientele of Redcar, Saltburn and Scarborough was from the north-east, including Scotland, whilst Hornsea, Withernsea and to some extent Bridlington were almost purely local resorts for Hull and East Yorkshire; the former two towns usually day trip destinations only.

By the 1870s the pleasure pier was firmly established an attraction for visitors to the seaside. Early piers such as Ryde (1814), Brighton Chain (1823) and Southend (1830) were built purely as landing stages, yet the Chain pier soon became popular as a superior promenade over the sea: a place to be seen, to breathe in the health-giving ozone-laden sea air, to walk upon the water without feeling seasick. To the delight of the pier's management, patrons were prepared to pay a handsome toll for the privilege of these benefits and to keep them amused further on the pier small shops, refreshment rooms, a telescope and a regimental band were provided.

The two Great Yarmouth piers of the 1850s, Britannia and Wellington, were amongst the first piers to be opened specifically for the use as promenades rather than as landing stages. Margate Jetty (1855), an iron pier erected by the prolific pier engineer Eugenius Birch, was a major breakthrough in pier design. The early wooden piers had suffered from continual attack from marine worms, but an iron pier, consisting of cast iron supporting columns, iron (or iron-sheathed wooden) piles, wrought iron ties, girders and bracing and wooden decking proved to be extremely durable, and became the blueprint design for many of the piers that followed. Birch ensured a solid foundation for the Margate pier by attaching a screw pile to the end of the columns to secure them into the beach.

Southport's iron pier of 1860 was celebrated as a promenade over the sea rather than just as a landing stage for boats; and heralded the start of the great pier-building era that saw nearly one hundred piers constructed over the next fifty years. The popularity of the resorts was increasing with the arrival of the railways, and the promotion of pier schemes was made simpler by the passing of the Piers & Harbours Act in 1861. Limited liability made it safer for shareholders to invest in a pier company; although many who invested in pier promotion and construction expecting to reap bumper benefits were to have their fingers burnt (especially at the smaller resorts). Sadly this was to prove the case with the six Yorkshire pleasure piers – Scarborough, Saltburn, Coatham, Redcar, Withernsea and Hornsea – which due to limited visitor numbers and consistent storm damage were never profitable and rarely paid a dividend to shareholders.

The Yorkshire resorts were quick off the ground with proposals for promenade piers. Schemes for Scarborough were afoot by the 1860s (with a pier being opened in 1868), as they were for Saltburn-by-the-Sea. Saltburn was being developed as a quiet, select resort by the Quaker Henry Pease and his Saltburn Improvement Company. The railway was extended to the town in 1861 and the plush Zetland Hotel was opened two years later. Work began on a pier in 1867 and it was opened two years later.

The Hornsea Pier Company was formed in 1865, although it was not until the following decade when a rival pier was planned that work on the pier actually commenced. The development of Hornsea as a small seaside resort was led by Joseph Armytage Wade, the so-called 'King of Hornsea', who brought the railway from Hull to the town in 1864. Armytage was also behind the formation of the Hornsea Pier Company, but the scheme lay dormant until a rival pier was promoted in 1875 by Sheffield businessmen Martin du Gillon. A bitter war of words ensued between the two men, with many locals supporting du Gillon's proposals above those of the autocratic Wade. The King of Hornsea eventually won the day and his pier was completed in 1880, yet his victory was to prove a pyrrhic one as disaster soon ensured that the pier spent all of its short, sad life in receivership.

Nearby Withernsea, an unpretentious resort popular with trippers from Hull, was also largely the creation of one man: Anthony Bannister, who formed the Withernsea Pier, Promenade, Gas & General Improvement Company. Bannister had brought the railway to the town from Hull in 1854 and had carried out a number of improvements including the construction of a promenade and sea wall. The pier was opened in 1877, yet its life was to be sadly as ill-fated as its compatriot at Hornsea.

Up on the Cleveland coast, the twin, but rival, resorts of Redcar and Coatham both built piers when one would have been clearly enough to serve both of them. The Redcar Pier Company was formed in 1866 but nothing was achieved until Coatham proposed a pier in 1870. Although joined at the hip and by a glorious stretch of sand the two towns had been developed with different aspirations. Redcar, despite being largely owned by Lord Zetland, also had a number of smaller freeholders and there was not the planned development of the resort as undertaken by the Newcomens, owners of Coatham. The development of the Cleveland iron trade led to Redcar housing a large number of working-class people employed in the industry. The town also had a small fishing fleet. The Newcomens began developing Coatham from 1860 with good quality villa and terrace accommodation. The seafront was enhanced with a new sea wall and promenade, and the resort also took on the guise of a Teeside commuter suburb. Coatham exuded a superior air to the more working-class Redcar, which was much resented in the latter. The differences in the two towns became focused in the provision of a pier for each of them. Work began on both piers in 1871 and Coatham became one of the earliest piers to include an integral pier pavilion/saloon as a feature. The piers of the 1860s and before were principally bare promenade decks with perhaps just a few kiosks and a bandstand. From the 1870s however, pavilions and saloons began to be built on new piers, or added to existing ones, to fight competition from land-based pavilions, theatres, aquaria and winter gardens. However, due to a lack of finance, pavilions were not to become a feature of the Yorkshire piers until much later. Scarborough Pier acquired a pavilion in 1889, yet Redcar did not acquire one until 1909 and Saltburn until 1929. Hornsea and Withernsea piers both initially boasted small pier head saloons (in reality little more than refreshment rooms) that quickly succumbed to the waves.

Pleasure piers would eventually come to offer all manner of varied amusements and entertainments; including orchestras, concert parties and plays in the pavilions, amusement machines and rides, roller skating rinks, open air dancing, divers, fishing and trips on paddle steamers. Of these, only Coatham Pier's roller skating rink, the concert parties and fishing were regular features of the cash-strapped Yorkshire piers (although Saltburn Pier now has an amusement arcade). Steamer trips from the Yorkshire piers were a rarity: poor berthing facilities due to insubstantial landing stages, rough sea conditions, and at Scarborough competition from an established harbour, meant that their landing stages were rendered quickly redundant.

Three of Yorkshire's principal resorts – Bridlington, Filey and Whitby – never built pleasure piers: two of them boasted fine harbour piers

An extremely busy North Harbour Pier at Bridlington c.1925. Marlinova Collection

popular for promenading whilst the other had a unique 'natural' pier. Nevertheless, both Bridlington and Filey had aborted pier schemes. Bridlington, Yorkshire's second biggest resort after Scarborough, had a fine harbour extensively redeveloped in the middle of the nineteenth century. Both the north and south piers were popular promenades and a pleasure pier would also have had to compete against a galaxy of other attractions the town had to offer, including the Spa Theatre, Grand Pavilion and Floral Pavilion.

Nevertheless, there were three attempts to provide a pleasure pier for Bridlington. In August 1880 it was proposed that a pier should be built out from the north end of the sea wall parade and in the following year it was announced that a company had been formed to build a 1,000ft iron pier opposite York Road. There was a further proposal for a pier in 1887. On 13 November 1899 the Bridlington Pier & Pavilion Company was incorporated with a capital of £40,000 comprising 40,000 £1 shares. The company was led by John and William Littlewood, renowned architects and engineers of Manchester, who had been involved in recent pier schemes at Morecambe and Colwyn Bay. Unfortunately their plan for Bridlington proved abortive and the company was finally dissolved on 20 November 1908 after having been inactive for many years.

Filey's 'natural' pier is the famous Brigg, a line of rocks that stretch for half a mile. The town had been developed as a resort from the 1830s and had acquired imposing cliff top terraces and crescents, along

Filey's natural pier, the Brigg, pictured on a postcard sent in 1906. Marlinova Collection

with gardens and a promenade. Filey became a small but select resort favoured by the upper middle classes. Such exclusivity meant proposals for a promenade pier (which would attract the masses) failed to find much favour. In 1873 the Filey Pier Company was formed, but had failed to register as a company with the Board of Trade by 24 August 1878. No business was ever carried out and the company was dissolved on 13 January 1885. The Filey Harbour Company fared no better. They were wound up in December 1883 after failing to gain support for a pier and harbour development. A proposed pier and tramway in 1890 also met with failure.

Whitby's fine stone harbour piers never encouraged a promenade pier development for the resort. Dating from around 1500, they were rebuilt in stone from the late eighteenth/early nineteenth century and timber extensions were added in 1910.

A pier was also never part of the proposals for Ravenscar, Yorkshire's 'resort that never was' which is situated on the south corner of Robin Hood's Bay where the Peak cliffs soar to an almost sheer 600ft above the sea. A West Riding development company acquired the land in 1896 to develop the area around the Raven Hall Hotel. A Marine Parade and hanging gardens were provided and a grid pattern of streets were laid out, but very little was ever built as only a few plots were sold. Even the special trains laid on to Ravenscar station failed to stir the buyers, and all that's left today is a terrace of shops by the derelict station, the

Whitby's fine harbour piers on a busy day in 1938. Marlinova Collection

The twin promenade decks of Hull Corporation Pier in 1909. Marlinova Collection

A postcard of the small pier at Paull, on which the sender has written: *Pier about 100 yards long the break you see is where a steamer ran into it one night.* Marlinova Collection

occasional house that was built and a few kerb stones indicating where the never completed roads would have furrowed. The main drawbacks to the development of Ravenscar were the 400ft descent to the beach and the exposure of the site to north-easterly gales.

Also worthy of mention is Hull's Corporation/Victoria Pier, a popular vantage point to watch the shipping in the River Humber. The first pier at Hull was erected in c.1801–3 for the ferry service to New Holland on the Lincolnshire side of the Humber. The pier was re-sited in 1834 and was extended to a length of 360ft. Difficulties over berthing at Hull led to the transfer of Humber services to the Corporation Pier in 1856. Erected in 1847, the pier was renamed the Victoria Pier in 1854 after it was used by Queen Victoria, although it was usually termed the Corporation Pier. An upper deck promenade was added to the pier in 1881–2, and in 1934 a pontoon replaced the old platforms. The ferry service to New Holland was finally ended on 24 June 1981 following the opening of the Humber Bridge. The pontoon was demolished the following year but the remainder of the pier was refurbished. The nearby Minerva Pier was mostly used for the landing and shipping of cargo.

Nearby Paull also once boasted a 300ft pier that was erected by the War Department in 1887 to replace an earlier pier built in 1866. Located opposite High Paul House, the pier was built in connection with a submarine mining establishment. The pier was damaged by a steamer in the early years of the twentieth century and was subsequently demolished.

Goole's Victoria Pier was strictly a commercial pier located in the dock area at the entrance to the lock. It has been rebuilt to a modern standard.

CHAPTER TWO

THE WHITE ELEPHANT OF THE NORTH BAY

SCARBOROUGH PIER, 1868–1905

As one of the country's leading seaside resorts, plans to provide a promenade pier for Scarborough were mooted in the early 1860s as the dawn of the great pier building era began.

The provision of a promenade pier was included in a grand scheme for the North Bay proposed by the Scarborough Pier & Improvement Company in 1862. The leading light behind the company was engineer Josiah Forster Fairbank, who had designed the sea water baths in South Bay and in 1861 had opened the Rock Gardens in the sparsely-developed North Bay. The gardens covered ten acres of the cliff side and were entered through a Moorish Temple opposite Rutland Street. A wooden assembly hall, with room to house up to 3,000 people (it was claimed), was provided for concerts and other entertainments.

In March 1862, the company issued their prospectus, which envisaged a capital of £20,000 (4,000 × £5 shares) for the scheme. The company was registered with the Board of Trade on 3 May 1862 and out of the 226 shares sold, 200 were held by Fairbank. In addition to a pier, there was to be a library and saloon on the sands, complete with hot and cold baths, a smoking room and refreshment refectory. A Hall of Crystal was also planned, to be fitted up for lectures and other intellectual enjoyments and studies. The centrepiece of the hall was to be the Great Globe of James Wyld MP, which was to be purchased at a twentieth of its original cost.

Once the scheme was complete, Fairbank announced that a tunnel was to be built through the castle headland linking the North and South Bays. However, in 1863, Fairbank's Rock Gardens were closed down because they were not sufficiently *au fait to claim the admiration and patronage of the fastidious*. This appeared to herald the end of Fairbank's ambitious plans for the North Bay and nothing further was heard of them. The Scarborough Pier & Improvement Company was finally dissolved on 7 March 1882.

In 1863, the Scarborough Marine Promenade & Jetty Company was formed to erect a pier in the South Bay. The pier was to be 1,410 feet long and 45 feet wide with a 225 × 90 feet pier head housing a saloon and refreshment rooms. A landing stage would allow use of the pier by

Scarborough Promenade Pier pictured shortly after it was fully opened in 1869. The pier head has a small refreshment saloon and landing steps. Courtesy of Scarborough Collectors Centre

Bathing machines front this view of Scarborough Pier taken during the 1870s. Marlinova Collection

boats at all states of the tide and moveable 6 feet high screens would prevent promenaders having to look down on bathers.

Unfortunately there was fierce opposition to the scheme not only that expected from the Scarborough Piers & Harbour Commissioners, but also from Scarborough Corporation and many townsfolk. One of them was even roused to comment:

> Some Goths are preparing to cut our beautiful bay in two with a pier. I'd have a big gun on St Nicholas Cliff well rammed with the whole scheme, and blow it to the waves.

However, in March 1864, the company was granted a provisional order by the Board of Trade to erect the pier. It was announced that shares were to be issued shortly, but they never were and no more was heard of the pier.

The third proposal for a promenade pier in Scarborough was initiated by a group of local bankers and merchants, including Major John Woodall-Woodall and William Henry Hammond of Raven Hall, Peak. The latter had originally suggested the scheme and held a meeting at the Queens Hotel, situated on the north side of the town where the pier was to be built. This led to the formation of the Scarborough Promenade Pier Company with a capital of £15,000 (3,000 × £5 shares), which in November 1865 issued its prospectus proposing a 1,000 feet pier.

Both Woodall and Hammond were influential and successful businessmen. Woodall was the eldest son of John Woodall, a banker and rich landowner in Scarborough who lived at St Nicholas House (now the Town Hall). He followed his father into the family's banking business of Woodall & Hebden and became as an influential Scarbronian as his father, serving on the Town Council from 1863-89 and holding office as mayor four times. Hammond was a Londoner who bought Raven Hall at Peak (later renamed Ravenscar in the 1890s) in 1841 as a summer residence. He was also the originator of the Scarborough & Whitby Railway that was to run through Peak. Eugenius Birch was engaged as engineer for the line and work was to have started in 1865, but lack of finance meant it was delayed until 1872. Unfortunately money troubles had halted construction by 1877. Four years later work started again with a new engineer, Sir Charles Fox and the line was finally opened on 16 July 1885. By then, Hammond (who had fathered seventeen children – eight dying in infancy) was an ill man and he died on 21 October 1885 aged eighty-three. His last resting-place, in Highgate Cemetery, London, lies close to that of Karl Marx.

Other directors of the company were named as Robert Forster, G Pirie, G F Brown and G Porritt. The company was registered with the Board of Trade on 1 December 1865 and in April 1866 they granted a provisional order for the pier's construction.

The company's decision to choose the design of Eugenius Birch for the pier was hardly a surprise, for as well as being involved with Hammond on the Scarborough & Whitby Railway, he had already designed piers at Margate, Blackpool (North), Deal, Brighton (West), Aberystwyth, Netley Hospital (Southampton) and Lytham. He went on to also lay out piers at New Brighton, Eastbourne, Hastings, Weston-super-Mare (Birnbeck), Bournemouth, Hornsea and Plymouth, as well as being involved in other works such as railways, harbours, aquaria and waterworks. However, outside the world of pier enthusiasts, his memory is now largely forgotten. No photograph of him has yet come to light and consequently Birch now comes across as a rather shadowy figure. The best account of his life is this obituary published in the minutes of proceedings of the Institution of Civil Engineers records following his death on 8 January 1884:

Birch, Eugenius was born in London in June 1818, his father being an architect and surveyor. He was educated at Brighton and at Euston Square. At a very early age he showed considerable mechanical and artistic talent, and was rarely seen without a pencil in his hand. He watched with much interest the cutting of the Regents Canal, and indeed frequently played truant to assist at the construction of the various great engineering works then in progress in the north of London, particularly the Primrose Hill tunnel of the London & Birmingham Railway. When quite a boy, he submitted a model of a railway carriage to the authorities of that line, who had offered a premium for an improvement in this direction, and the Greenwich Railway Company at once adopted his mode of putting wheels under the carriages. At the age of sixteen, being then employed at Messrs Bligh's engineering works, Limehouse, Eugenius Birch planned a marine steam engine, which so pleased Dr George Birkbeck, that the latter strongly advised the youth to join the local Mechanics Institute. This he did, and to such purpose that, the master falling ill, he undertook the entire charge of the drawing classes for some time, to the satisfaction of all concerned. In 1837, he received a Silver Isis Medal from the Society of Arts for his drawing of a marine steam-engine, and in the following year a Silver Telford Medal and a premium of books from this institution for his drawings and description of Huddart's rope-machinery. This subject was continued in a subsequent communication descriptive of a 'machine for sew flat ropes' for which he likewise received a premium.

The encouragement thus given seems to have determined Mr Birch to adopt the profession of a civil engineer. On the 19th February 1839, he was elected a

Graduate of the Institution, in which class he remained till he was transferred as a member on the 5th May 1863, and shortly afterwards he entered into partnership with his elder brother, the late Mr John Brannis Birch. He was actively engaged in works of varied character until 1845, when the Railway Mania absorbed his whole faculties. On the bursting of the railway bubble in England, Mr Birch and his brother were engaged in laying out the East Indian Railway from Calcutta to Delhi, designing the whole of the bridges and viaducts, and it was upon the material thus furnished that the guarantee of the line was obtained. Between 1847 and 1851, he designed and carried out the Kelham and Stockwith bridges in Nottinghamshire. But Mr Birch's claims to recognition are chiefly based upon the system of promenade piers which he and his brother initiated, and which now form a feature of nearly every watering-place on the English Coast.

The first, and for many years, single example of the screw pile, was the well-known Margate Jetty, which was completed in 1853 [sic – it was actually started that year, completion was in 1857], and formed a new departure in marine construction. It was from the first a most successful work, and has since been considerably improved and extended. Similar piers were subsequently erected from Mr Birch's designs at Aberystwyth, Blackpool, Bournemouth, Brighton (West), Deal, Eastbourne, Hastings, Hornsea, Lytham, New Brighton, Plymouth, Scarborough and other places. However, these only form part of many extensive works of improvement. Mr Eugenius Birch was also the first to construct a large seawater aquarium with recreational adjuncts. Of those such buildings, those at Brighton and Scarborough are types which have been followed at many other watering-places. The tanks were of much larger dimensions than those previously used, and their construction involved some interesting problems on the pressure of water against large surfaces, and the thickness of material [glass] required to stand it.

But though provision for the delectation of visitors to the seaside formed a large part of Mr Birch's business, it was by no means the whole of it. He carried out the Devon and Somerset Railway, the Exmouth Docks, Ilfracombe Harbour, the West Surrey Waterworks, and was the first engineer of the Scarborough and Whitby Railway, which he laid out, although the construction of the works was for long in abeyance and is now being completed by other parties. His last great design was for a Marine Kursaal to be erected at the end of the Chain Pier, Brighton, for which Parliamentary sanction had been obtained, but he did not live to carry out this important work. The design represents a huge ship arranged and fitted-up as a first class hotel.

Had he not chosen to be an engineer, he might have risen to eminence as an artist, being possessed of high talent in that direction. The beauty of his drawings of Huddart's rope machinery, submitted when he was a Graduate, attracted considerable attention and the artistic faculty remained with him through life. During a tour of Italy, Egypt, and Nubia in the winter of 1874-5, he made a series of more than a hundred watercolour drawings and sketches of such merit that a special exhibition was made of them. After his death, these drawings realised high prices, being assisted, no doubt by the interest felt at the time in all concerning Egypt. Mr Birch was a pleasant and genial companion, and a thoroughly honourable man. He died after a long and painful illness on 8th January 1884.

The Scarborough Promenade Pier Company accepted the tender of £12,135 submitted by J E Dowson, of London, to build the pier. Dowson was a regular Birch contractor, having worked (or who was working) on his piers at Aberystwyth (1864-5), New Brighton (1866-7) and Eastbourne (1866-72), the latter simultaneously under construction at the same time as Scarborough Pier. In addition he erected Bognor Pier (1864-5) for Joseph Wilson.

The first pile of the pier was driven in on 14 September 1866, following which the guest party made their way up the cliff to the Queens Hotel for luncheon. The ceremony was described in a local newspaper as:

> Yesterday, according to the previous announcement, the first pile of the promenade pier was driven in by the Chairman of the Company, Major Woodall, and our best hopes are that no disturbing cause may ever remove it from the position it then took.
>
> At the appointed hour of 12 o'clock yesterday the Chairman and a large party of the gentry of the town, comprising the projectors and shareholders of the Company, the Borough Magistrates, the Members of the Town Council, and the public, assembled at the Town Hall, whence they proceeded to the site of the proposed pier. Here an animated scene presented itself. The men of the coastguard were drawn up, and at a given signal the capstan bars forming the appliance by which the pile was to be screwed into its bed, were driven round and the work was declared to be satisfactorily performed.

The pier was to be 1,000 feet long and 23 feet wide terminating in a 140 × 50 feet pier head. The wooden deck would be supported by continuous iron girders and wrought iron bracing atop thirteen clusters of cast iron columns and wooden screw piles, in spans of 66 feet. The deck accommodated six pairs of recesses, each with a width of 35 feet, and continuous seating. The pier head rested upon sixty-two wrought iron columns and piles, formed of Barlow rails and similar to those used on Birch's Deal Pier. A saloon was to be placed on the head for band concerts and refreshments, and landing inclines (but no landing stage) would allow steamers and pleasure craft to call.

On 26 January 1867, the area of the pier head beyond the low water mark was conveyed to the pier company. In the following month, Birch reported to the company that *a large quantity of the cast iron columns is on the ground* (but presumably not in it) *and nearly all the timber is delivered.* Perhaps the company had inquired why so little of the pier had yet been built, but it is known the contractors were having difficulty in fixing the columns due to the rocky foundations. Furthermore, rough seas were regularly grinding the work to a halt. The worst occasion was in November 1867 when storms caused damage to the unfinished structure.

In 1867, the company, already in the process of building a new road down to the pier from Queens Parade, also put forward a proposal to erect a road around the Castle Headland to connect the North and South bays. The plans never got off the drawing board, although the Marine Drive was eventually built in 1908.

By March 1868, some 800 feet of the pier had been completed; however, the death of Dowson led to both Scarborough and Eastbourne Piers being finished by Head Wrightson. Based at the Teesdale Ironworks, Thornaby-on-Tees, Stockton, they were one of Britain's leading engineering contractors. The firm dated back to 1840 and at their height employed 1700 men on their various works, plus another 300 engaged on erecting sites. Altogether, they were to construct ten piers: in addition to Scarborough and Eastbourne, they were Redcar (1871–3), Cleethorpes (1872–3), Southsea South Parade (1878-9), Skegness (1879–81), Ramsgate (1879–81), Ramsey (1882–6), St Leonards (1889–91) and Herne Bay (1896–9).

However, by the time Head Wrightson had taken over construction of the pier, the pier company had only raised £9,635 of the total cost and the contractors were fretting that they were not going to be paid. This perhaps accounts for the fact that when the pier was opened to the public on Monday, 17 August 1868 (when 900 feet long with the pier head to be completed) the money gained from the 2,000–3,000 people who paid a 1d toll to walk on it went to Head Wrightson. The final cost of construction of the pier was said to be around £15,000.

The full 1,000 feet of the pier was finally opened to the public on 1 May 1869, who were charged 1d entrance fee. However, the official opening day was delayed until 5 July 1869 (perhaps to ensure all works were complete) when the North Eastern Railway agreed to run special excursion trains from Yorkshire, Lancashire and Derbyshire to coincide with the opening. Two military bands, the 15th Hussars (conducted by Herr Hartmann) and the 2nd West York Light Infantry (conducted by Mr Fender) were engaged to play on the pier. Unfortunately, a thunderstorm meant the pier had a *small and disheartening patronage.*

The North Cliff seen from the Scarborough Pier c.1885. The short-lived Queens Parade Tramway (1878–87) can be seen on the cliff side. Marlinova Collection

Although the opening day of the pier may have been a disappointment, the remainder of the 1869 season proved to be a success as £536 was taken in tolls. Receipts took a dip in 1870 when only £417 was gathered in, but 1871 (£552) and 1873 (£580) were both quite successful enabling small dividends to be paid to shareholders (which included Messrs Head, Wrightson and Birch). However, the company remained in debt, with £2,000 being owed to Woodall & Hebden's Bank. Furthermore, the frequent repairs carried out to the pier following storm damage were eroding the company's finances. One such occasion was in February 1877 when during a storm the whole structure was submerged. Half the deck was sprung by the waves and joists, planks and four lamps were swept away. The pier head was also damaged. Part of the blame has to lie with Birch, who designed the pier too 'low' and miscalculated the height of spring tides and stormy seas. He made the same mistake at Margate and Eastbourne (where half the pier was washed away in 1877), while Brighton West and Blackpool North (which had to be heightened during construction) both needed strengthening.

The pier also suffered damage from collisions by the few ships that tried to call at the pier head. It had been hoped visiting steamers would be a regular feature, attracting more visitors and bringing in extra revenue, but the lack of a landing stage precluded this. Eventually all ships were forbidden to call.

By 1875, visitor numbers to the pier were already in decline (in the following year, 1876, they amounted to £491) and this was put down to its isolated position and the fact it could only be reached by a steep, winding road down the cliff. One proposal to improve access was to construct a cliff tramway and in 1875 Woodall suggested such a scheme. However the Scarborough Queens Parade Tramway Company, with a capital of £3,500, eventually built the tramway. A design by Henry Holt of Leeds was accepted and various contractors, including Messrs. Wade of Leeds, built the structure. The 4-foot gauge line ran for 218 feet on an average gradient of 1 in 2.3. The two cars, operated on the water-balance principle, could carry up to fourteen passengers each. The upper station was located near the summit of the pier approach road and was open to the elements, although there was a hut for the brakeman. From there, the track ran down along iron girders through a tunnel and then a cutting before reaching the lower station. This was located by the pier entrance and housed the ticket office and a waiting room for up to forty passengers. A 3½-hp gas engine pumped the water from a brick tank under the station.

The tramway had an auspicious start when one of the cars ran loose during testing, but in October 1878 it was opened to the public.

Sadly, the provision of the tramway failed to make a noticeable difference to the numbers visiting the pier. In 1878, receipts fell to just £361 7s 9d (the opening of the aquarium was said to be a factor), although an increase in the admission charge to 2d increased takings to £395 16s 3d in 1879. The company was no longer paying a dividend (only to some preference shareholders) and was in serious financial trouble as £823 was still owed to the bank. However, the situation continued to worsen and the annual report for 1882 stated that there were gross receipts of just £316 2s 11d for the year, a decrease of £2 12s 7d on the £318 15s 11d acquired in 1881, notwithstanding admission to the pier had been reduced back to 1d. Furthermore, a crippling £412 12s 6d had to be paid out to Tillotson & Son of Leeds during 1881–2 for repairs to the pier head. In a bid to keep down expenses, it was decided to close the pier during the winter months.

Yet, regrettably, matters took a further turn for the worse on Wednesday, 22 August 1883, when in dense fog, the steam trawler *Star*, belonging to W H Shawcross of Scarborough and under the control of Master Ledley, ran into the middle of the pier on the north side. Two of the iron columns were knocked down and lamps and bulwarks were damaged.

Repairs were estimated to cost between £100–200. The vessel had her mast carried away, but otherwise sustained little damage.

Incredibly, on Friday 14 September 1883, less than a month after the *Star* collision, the steam vessel *Hardwick* also ran aground against the pier. Belonging to Ropner & Co of Hartlepool, the 750-ton vessel left London three days earlier in ballast, but was run into by the *Croesus* in thick fog off Flamborough Head. Fireman John Hennessey was sadly a fatality. The *Hardwick* was taken in tow by the *Croesus* bound for West Hartlepool, but heavy seas led the master of the *Hardwick* to part with the hawser. A Scarborough steam trawler then agreed to tug the stricken vessel to its home port and ran it aground in the North Bay close to the pier. Unfortunately the incoming tide floated the ship against the pier, knocking down three columns.

The year 1883 had one more nasty shock in store for the pier, when in December a severe gale blew the band shelter clean off the pier head. The pier remained un-repaired and suffered further damage when the yacht *Escalpa* crashed into it one winter's night.

Things continued to go from bad to worse. In 1886 receipts amounted to only £211 and following a landslip, the Queens Parade Tramway was closed in August 1887, never to reopen. The tramway had been plagued by landslips and mishaps during its short life and proved to be a financial disaster. The operating company were only too pleased to sell it to Scarborough Corporation, who totally removed all trace of it so the area could be incorporated into the new Clarence Gardens, which opened in 1890.

The 1888 season yielded only £175 in gate receipts and this proved to be the final straw that broke the camel's back. Woodall, who had proposed winding up the company the previous year, announced that Woodall & Hebden's Bank would no longer support the pier financially. This led to the Scarborough Promenade Pier company being wound up on 25 January 1889 with the statement *it has been proved to the satisfaction of the shareholders of the Company that the Scarborough Promenade Pier Co. Ltd cannot by reason of its liabilities continue its business and that it is advisable to wind up the same.* Mr James Pirie, Secretary of the company, was appointed liquidator and a final meeting was held on 19 July 1889 in order to settle the Company's affairs, when it was stated there was an overdraft of £1,343.

Scarborough Corporation, who in addition to laying out the Clarence Gardens was building the Royal Albert Drive along the North Bay foreshore, was offered the pier, but declined. The pier was then put up for sale by public auction on Saturday, 31 March 1889 where it was stated the saloon had a six day full liquor licence and was rented out at

An 1891 view of Scarborough North Pier showing the enlarged refreshment room on the pier head and the pavilion at the entrance both added in 1889. Marlinova Collection

A closer view of the pier head refreshment room. Judging by the parasols, it must have been a warm day. Marlinova Collection

£40 per annum. The refreshment room at the entrance was rented by the Scarborough Coffee House Company at a cost of £17 10s per annum.

The pier was purchased by George Ernest Hudson (known as Walter Hudson) of London for only £1,240 who formed the Scarborough North Pier Company with a capital of £13,000. The company announced that a new building was to be erected at the entrance to the pier and a larger one on the pier head, to plans prepared by architects Hall & Tugwell. The new entrance building was to incorporate the existing kiosks and include two 36 feet turrets at each end, along with an 18-foot archway leading to an artiste arcade. A refreshment room, concert room and shops would also be provided. The pier itself was to be strengthened by Messrs Appleby & Brogden of Sandside and lit with electricity. The total cost of the work was estimated at £4,000.

On August Bank Holiday 1889, the pier was reopened with Mr Quinton Gibson's Band playing in the new recreation room. However, the works to the pier were not finished and the *catering arrangements were by no means in a complete state, which created a little confusion and dissatisfaction.* The new 'Grand Pavilion' staged variety entertainment at 3 p.m. and vocal and instrumental concerts every evening at 7.30. On Sundays sacred concerts were held. An entertaining diver, W S Johnson, amused the crowd with his antics and bathing under the pavilion was available from 7am to noon. Winter fishing tickets, covering the period October to March, cost 10/6. One disappointment for the new pier owners however was the Scarborough Brewster Sessions refusal to allow the transfer of the liquor licence from the pier head saloon to the new refreshment room at the pier entrance.

The year 1890 saw the completion of Scarborough Corporation's revamp of the North Bay, which included the Royal Albert Drive, a new sea wall and the Clarence Gardens. The work, which had begun in 1886, cost a total of £50,000. The gardens, named in honour of the Duke of Clarence who formally opened the Royal Albert Drive, had as its centrepiece Flagstaff Hill, reached via a rustic wooden bridge. The gardens also had winding paths, secluded nooks and crannies and a bandstand. Entertainment in the gardens, which included military bands and pierrot shows, was sometimes sponsored by the North Bay boarding house keepers.

These improvements to the North Bay, along with the alterations to the pier itself, boded well for an upturn in fortune. Quinton Gibson 'The Greatest Lady Impersonator in the World' was engaged to organise variety concerts in the new pavilion and he hired all manner of weird and wonderful acts. In 1891 these included (as well as Gibson himself) George Burnley on piano, the Great Duprez – Monarch of Magicians &

The entrance building to Scarborough Pier, which housed a concert room, shops and refreshment facilities. Marlinova Collection

A look along the almost deserted deck of the pier c.1890. Marlinova Collection

His Educated Dogs, Miss Lilian Taylor's Anglo-Swiss Choir, Professor Grantham – England's Singing Ventriloquist and Herbert Albini – the only original King of Cards & Royal Court Wizard.

Gibson and the Great Duprez were still performing on the pier three years later when William Morgan was appointed manager. Morgan was a big player in Scarborough and had proven managerial experience in the entertainment world. He ran the Scarborough Aquarium; and in 1879–86 was manager of Blackpool Winter Gardens. During his time there, he attempted to bring in entertainments more suitable for Blackpool's growing number of middle and working class visitors but met with opposition from the Board of Directors. Morgan styled the pier shows 'Refined Drawing Room Entertainments', and in addition to the 2d entrance toll, an additional 2d was charged for the shows (front seats were 3d extra).

Morgan was retained for the 1895 season and his 'Grand Entertainments over the Sea' included the North Pier Orchestra (under the direction of George Burnley), Mademoiselle Lurline – Champion High Diver and Oceanus, a champion tank performer.

By 1898 the orchestra had been dispensed with and Dryden's Variety Concerts and Dances were the main feature. There were two shows daily, at 3.30pm and 7.30pm, and admission was 6d (including pier toll). Supporting acts for the season included:

Fred Percy – The world's Greatest Negro Impersonator
Tom Lloyd – Great Yorkshire Comedian
Miss Nita Meyer – 'up to date variety entertainment'
Horace Gibb – Descriptive Vocalist
Miss Rosie Irving – Charming Vocalist
The Scarborough Rifle Volunteer Band
H.E. High – Tramp Skater
Belle Whitehead – Skirt Dancer
Cinematograph & Gramophone

For the 1899 season, the pier entertainments were placed under the direct management of the Company. They went upmarket by staging high-class concerts (6d including pier toll) featuring operatic sopranos and baritones. However this appears not to have been a beneficial move, for in 1900 it was reported *Mr G. Egerton Burnett is working hard to bring the pier to the height of success which it has not attained in previous seasons.*

In 1901, a Mr Platts was named as Manager and Secretary of the Scarborough North Pier Company, during another unsuccessful attempt by the company to transfer the alcohol licence from the pier

The pier forms a backdrop to this delightful photograph of children paddling in the North Bay at low tide c.1900. Courtesy of Scarborough Collectors Centre

A further view of the pier at low tide, showing a side view of the pier head refreshment room. Courtesy of Scarborough Collectors Centre

Looking down onto the pier from the cliff c.1902 with a choppy sea in evidence and not many people on the pier. Courtesy of Scarborough Collectors Centre

The pier looks busier in this view taken c.1904. Note the lettering on the pavilion roof 'Variety Entertainments During Weekdays' and 'Sacred Concerts Afternoon & Evening on Sundays'. Courtesy of Scarborough Collectors Centre

head saloon to the pier entrance building. The Board of Directors at the time was listed as G E Hudson, brewer; Cyrus Holliday, colliery owner; Charles Gott, civil engineer and William Holton, manufacturer (Hudson resigned however in 1902 and was replaced by William Morgan). The season's entertainment for 1901 was low-key, with just a ladies orchestra provided for the morning and the Borough Brass Band every Sunday.

On Saturday, 21 November 1903, the pier was damaged by a severe north to north-westerly gale, coupled with a high tide. Around 200 feet of the decking was torn up at the shore end and a quantity of ironwork was destroyed along both sides of the pier. A number of windows in the café at the entrance were also broken; and the damage all told amounted to about £200. Several anglers were trapped on the pier head during the storm and had to be rescued by boat.

The directors of the company proposed making a storm claim against Scarborough Corporation. They alleged that the new sea wall had caused a backlash of the sea during the gale and that this had contributed to the damage suffered by the pier. However they were in no financial position to go ahead with the claim and on 2 January 1904 William Holton resigned as a director of the company. In April 1904, the company went into liquidation, having vainly tried, but failed, to make a go of 'Scarborough's White Elephant'.

The pier was put up for auction on 21 September 1904 and it was acquired for £3,500 by its former manager (and now Scarborough's mayor) William Morgan. He announced that he was to spend £5,000 on improvements to the structure, including raising the deck by 6–8 feet to lessen its damage by stormy seas and erecting a landing stage. A new cliff lift to the pier and a bathing pool were also part of the plans. For the 1905 season the tolls and bar were to be let at a rental of £450.

The year 1905 was welcomed in stormy fashion on the north-east coast and in Scarborough's North Bay; the promenade pier took its usual winter battering. The nights of Friday 6 and Saturday 7 January were particularly tempestuous and the consequences for the pier were fatal, as reported in the *Scarborough Mercury*:

> The full force of the gale was felt in the North Bay, where enormous damage was done. The exceptionally high tide, coupled with the combination of a gale of wind from the north-west and a backwash from the Royal Albert Drive, completely swept away practically the whole of the promenade pier. The whole of the promenade decking between the entrance and the pavilion at the far end was torn away like matchwood, and this morning all that was to be seen was one long girder lying on the sands, the tide being about halfway out. Along the North Foreshore the woodwork could be seen strewn all over

During on 7 January 1905 Scarborough Pier was almost totally wrecked, leaving just the entrance and pier head buildings standing. The sender of this postcard wrote: *Wreck of the North Pier in the gale of Friday, which is more complete than it looks here.* Marlinova Collection

the roadway; most of it having been broken into matchwood. Workmen were early on the scene clearing away the wreckage and his worship the mayor (the owner of the pier), having been informed of the disaster, was soon on the scene. The main entrance to the pier on Royal Albert Drive was seriously damaged, the windows and a considerable portion of the woodwork being smashed and the flooring torn up. Three iron uprights supported the end nearest the sea, in which direction it projected some yards and the opinion was generally expressed that unless supported very soon it would collapse. It was impossible to reach the pavilion, which alone was left standing, but it could be seen that the iron supports of this had been dislodged. Some were bent, others appeared to have been washed completely away, whilst at the shore end of the pavilion proper, the wooden portion had gone, leaving the bar exposed to view. The larger portions of the woodwork that have been washed onto the foreshore have considerably damaged the railings and the sight presented to those early on the scene this morning was one of complete and utter ruin.

The newspaper went on to say that damage to the pier was an annual occurrence, the last serious occasion being the night of Saturday, 21 November 1903. Redcar Pier also suffered damage when a girder

A snapshot of the entrance building following the storm showing the point where the pier deck broke off and fell into the sea. Marlinova Collection

An unusual photograph of the interior damage sustained by the pier entrance building. Courtesy of Scarborough Collectors Centre

on the west side of the pier head was displaced and decking was torn up.

On hearing of the disaster, local photography firms such as Thomas Taylor, E T W Dennis and others (many of whom did not record their names on the cards they produced), rushed to the pier to record the scene. The photographs they took were quickly reproduced as picture postcards (in some cases on the same day), which were eagerly snapped up by the public as mementoes of the occasion. It was ironically commented that the only time the pier made anyone any money was after its destruction!

Due to its history of storm damage, the pier could not be insured and Morgan quickly decided it would be unwise to rebuild it in view of its unprofitable past. The iron lying on the North Bay sands was sold off to Messrs F Goodwill and Castle House, both of Scarborough, for £500. Morgan's lessee of the pier, Bertie Whitaker, had just taken it on at £300 for the year, which was not returnable! However, he continued to run the shore end building until his lease ran out. Whitaker was a successful businessman, involved in catering, motor cars, manufacturing, furnishings and entertainment.

The pier head pavilion isolated in the bay was not carted off as scrap along with the rest of the pier. This was because it held the pier's liquor licence, which Morgan did not want to lose. Yet past applications to have the licence transferred to the shore end building had all failed, so it was suggested perhaps a cable car could connect the two ends of the pier to enable the pavilion to still function! Morgan however decided to apply once more to transfer the licence to the shore end, much to the chagrin of local temperance movements. The *Scarborough Mercury* of 10 February 1905 reported:

> The North Pier Licence Application: At a meeting of the Executive Committee of the Scarborough Free Church Council, it was decided to approach the Bishop of Hull with a view to his joining a deputation to wait upon the licensing justices at the Brewster Sessions next week to urge upon the justices the advisability of refusing to comply with the application of the transfer of the licence of the North Promenade Pier from the pavilion end to the entrance portion.

At the Brewster Sessions, Morgan stated that an entertainment room 15 feet wide × 66 feet long and seating 100, was to be provided in the entrance building and an adjoining café would greatly benefit from holding a liquor licence. However the application to transfer the licence was refused, and furthermore, on 10 March 1905, it was taken

A crowd watches a stormy sea lash the promenade and surviving pier entrance building c.1910. The building became dilapidated and was demolished in January 1914. Marlinova Collection

away altogether on the grounds it was no longer needed due to the inaccessibility of the pier head pavilion. This decision meant there was no longer any reason for Morgan to retain the pavilion and on Friday, 11 August 1905 the *Scarborough Mercury* reported: *The old pavilion disappeared on Wednesday morning.*

On 15 July 1905, Morgan made good his promise at the Brewster Sessions (in spite of the loss of the liquor licence) by opening a new concert hall in the surviving pier entrance building. The hall was entered directly from the Royal Albert Drive and could seat 400. On 29 July, Mr Victor Stevens' Premier Pierrot Operatic & Variety Concert Party began a month's engagement. Three performances were given daily at 11.30, 3.00 & 7.30, with a Sunday concert at 8.00. In addition to the concert hall, the entrance building also housed a refreshment room and shops.

For the 1906 season, William Morgan was in charge of the hall himself and amongst his engagements were Mr Charles Morritt and the Excelsior Opera Singers. In 1907, Wilfred Ellerslie was engaged as manager. He provided a fare of mainly vaudeville artists such as comediennes, conjurors, singers and burlesque sketches. There were also 'Pierograph Animated Pictures' and free sacred concerts on Sundays.

The concert hall was not advertised from the 1908 season onwards and presumably it went out of use. The building became shabby, but nevertheless still continued to hold out against the force of a stormy North Bay high tide. Scarborough Corporation however, was keen for it to go and on 2 January 1914 applied to borrow £1,150 for the purchase and demolition of the 'North Pier entrance buildings'. This was to cover the £600 purchase price and £550 demolition costs. The building was described as being in a dilapidated condition and an eyesore. The demolition was completed by April 1914 and a suitable epitaph was penned by the *Scarborough Pictorial*:

> The passing of Scarborough Pier has left the sea to be free once again to lash itself in fury against the Royal Albert Drive wall; washing gleefully over the foundations of what once had to meet the full force of the oncoming waves and was, to all intents and purposes, destroyed for daring to offer resistance!

Surviving pile foundations of Scarborough Promenade Pier, 2001. Marlinova Collection

Chapter Three
The Doughty Survivor

A small village (if it may be called) about five miles and half east of Redcar and three miles eastward of Markse, consists of a few houses at the foot of the Huntcliffe rocks, the best road to which is on the sands. Here is a small but clean inn to which many of the visitors at Redcar resort, where, after their ride or walk, they may enjoy a treat of tea and 'fat rascals', and those who visit Saltburn for pleasures of a different description – such as beautifully romantic scenery and magnificently extensive sea views – will find themselves amply repaid if they ascend to the top of the cliffs.

That was W Harrison of Ripon's description in 1841 of the old village of Saltburn, nestled around the Ship Inn under the Huntcliff, the most northerly headland of the rocky Yorkshire coast.

The village was to remain a small isolated settlement until it was espied by Quaker Henry Pease during a visit to his brother who lived at Cliff House, Markse. Pease was said to have seen *in a sort of prophetic vision, on the edge of the cliff before him, a town arise and the quiet unfrequented glen turned into a lovely garden.*

Saltburn Pier nearing completion in 1869 with its full original length of 1,500ft. Note the piles stored on the promenade. Courtesy of the late Norman Bainbridge

Pease was Member of Parliament for South Durham and an influential businessman with a finger in many pies. In addition to being a board member of the Stockton & Darlington Railway, he was involved with the Darlington Iron Company, Stockton & Middlesbrough Water Company, Weardale & Shildon Water Company, South Durham & Lancashire Union Railway and Pease & Partners, the family's own brickworks. Pease was also Darlington's first mayor, and as chairman of the Peace Society travelled throughout Europe in a bid to halt impending conflicts.

Pease thought that the area around the old village would make an attractive bathing resort with its wooden ravine, cliff scenery and fine sandy beach. He also foresaw a profitable business proposition with the wealthy of the north east staying at select hotels at the resort, whilst those of a more modest means stayed in boarding houses tucked away in the streets behind the front.

An extension of the railway from Redcar to Saltburn received the Royal Assent in 1858 and in the following year Pease formed the Saltburn Improvement Company (SIC) to build the new resort of Saltburn-by-the-Sea. The land was acquired from the local landowner Lord Zetland and Henry Pease laid the foundation stone of the new town on 23 January 1861.

The layout of the resort was entrusted to George Dickenson of Darlington, the winner of a £50 design competition. However, the path of the railway through the centre of the proposed development presented an awkward problem and limited its scope. The railway was opened on 17 August 1861 and two years later became part of the North Eastern Railway system.

The SIC stipulated that the majority of the new town must be constructed of white firebrick, manufactured at Pease's own works![1] In addition Westmorland slate would have to be used to tile the roofs.

On 27 July 1863, Lord Zetland opened the stylish hotel that bore his name and in the following year the Valley Gardens in Saltburn Glen were laid out, complete with its own natural health-giving spring. The Ha'penny Bridge across the Glen, so called because there was a ½d toll to use it, was opened in 1869.

By 1865, Saltburn-by-the-Sea had one hundred houses, along with a Wesleyan chapel and an ornate water tower. The latter however was only in use for two years and was demolished in 1905.

The new resort was romantically described in *The Watering Places of Cleveland* (1869):

Upon emerging from the station, the visitor finds that Saltburn is composed of several clean and well-built streets, whose shops and houses present a

The pier and hoist c.1870. The wooden hoist was built to enable easy access to the pier from the town. Designed by John Anderson the hoist had a single cage that could carry twenty passengers up and down the 120ft drop. It was worked using the counterbalance principle of using water to fill a tank to descend it to the bottom, and then emptying the tank to allow it to go back up. The fare was 1d up and 1½ down. Marlinova Collection

respectable, airy and cheerful appearance; and he maybe inclined to think that some lapidary, the names of Ruby Street, Pearl Street, Amber Street, Diamond Street, Emerald Street and Garnet Street. The situation of Saltburn is exceedingly eligible as a marine resort, as it occupies an eminence of about 150 feet high, overlooking the North Sea, and is surrounded by various magnificent scenery; comprising precipitous cliffs hundreds of feet in height, one of the most extensive and excellent of sandy beaches to be found on the British coast, with many acres of ground laid out in a perfect paradise of gardens, and vast glens whose wild beauty calls up the imagination the most brilliant description of the luxuriance of tropical climes. The tide gently laves the sandy beach below us, and fills the air with a murmur almost musical as it falls upon the ear. Before us lie snugly in the valley a few cottages – all that is left of the old Saltburn – but whose position, sheltered by the neighbouring hills, is highly picturesque.

One of the principal developers of the land put on the market by the SIC was John Anderson, and in January 1867 he was appointed resident engineer of the company. Anderson opened his own one hundred room hotel (the Alexandra) and in October 1867 formed the Saltburn-by-the-Sea Pier Company, for which he was both engineer and contractor.

No time was wasted in getting the pier started and in December 1867 Cochrane & Grove of Ormesby Foundry delivered the first consignment of ironwork. The first pile was driven in by Mrs Thomas Vaughan of Gunnergate Hall on 27 January 1868 and on 6 April 1868 the Board of Trade granted a Provisional Order for the construction of the pier. The land and foreshore for the pier were conveyed to the company on 3 July 1868, although by that time, much of the pier had been constructed below the high water mark.

In May 1869 the pier was opened to the public, and to ease access to it from the town above, a 120ft high wooden vertical hoist, designed by John Anderson, was provided. Both the new pier and hoist were described in *The Watering Places of Cleveland*:

> Hitherto Saltburn has been accessible to visitors coming seaward only through the inconvenient and, at times, dangerous mode of disembarkation by means of small boats. To obviate this, a company was formed for the erection of a pier, available for the landing or embarkation of passengers at any state of the tide. This pier, which is now built, is a light elegant structure of cast iron, one thousand five hundred feet in length and twenty-five feet in breadth, and it forms an admirable promenade. In the centre are shops for the sale of refreshments, and at the end, a saloon in which persons, even those in the most delicate of health, may sit and enjoy the sea breezes without the slightest inconvenience.[2] At the shore end is a hoist for the raising and lowering of people, thus avoiding the toilsome ascent by the road.

The pier proved to be an immediate success and over 50,000 people paid to stroll upon it during its first six months. This enabled a 4½% dividend for shareholders to be announced at the first AGM of the company at the Alexandra Hotel on 26 March 1870.

On 14 May 1870, two steamers operated a service from the pier to Middlesbrough whilst a band performed on the pier head. In the following month there were further steamer trips to Middlesbrough and Hartlepool and an excursion aboard the *Victor* to Scarborough. Further revenue was gained from letting advertising space on the pier at 5s per annum. A successful season enabled the pier company to announce a 10% dividend at its half yearly meeting on 15 October 1870.

There were further dividends of 6% in 1871 and 1¾% in 1873. At the half yearly meeting of the company in October 1873 it was announced that all its shares had been disposed off. John Anderson had been paid

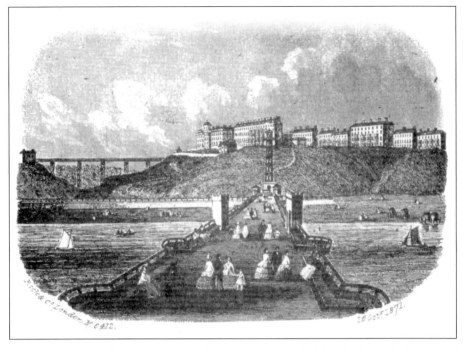

An engraving of the pier in 1872, showing two castle-like kiosks which housed small shops. In the distance can be seen the hoist and Ha'penny Bridge. Marlinova Collection

£500 of the £2,000 owed, and although there was £201 of disposable income, £2,500 was needed to erect a saloon and other buildings at the end of the pier (as originally intended) and provide gas lighting along the pier.

The following year (1874) also proved to be reasonably successful and a dividend of 4½% was paid. At Whitsun 1875 it was reported that *the whole stretch of 1,500ft promenade appeared to be literally alive all day.* Unfortunately, disaster struck during the night of 21/22 October 1875 when a stormy sea washed away 300ft of the sea end of the pier. It was claimed that the action of marine worms had considerably weakened the timber built landing stage.

The company decided that the lost section of the pier, along with the landing stage (which had rarely been used) was not to be rebuilt, although it was hoped to widen the pier to give the same walking area (not actually carried out). To pay for repairs, the company had to borrow £3,000 at 4% interest from the SIC; who themselves were facing financial difficulties as the development of the town had temporarily halted due to a slump in the Teeside iron trade.

Saltburn Pier in c.1880 after it had been rebuilt to a shorter length of 1,250ft following storm damage in 1875. Courtesy of the late Norman Bainbridge

During the reconstruction of the pier in 1876–7, a new pier head was built onto the end of the shortened pier, onto which a bandstand and sheltered seating were added in 1884. Courtesy of the late Norman Bainbridge

At the company's half-yearly meeting on 13 November 1876, it was announced that repairs to the pier were progressing favourably and dynamite was being used to remove iron piles from the wrecked sea end of the pier. The pier was reopened the following year after being strengthened to a reduced length of 1,250ft. A new pier head was built onto structure at a higher level. At the end of the season a 1% dividend was paid to shareholders. However, the heavy debt incurred by the company led it to be wound up in December 1879.

Eventually, on 30 August 1883, the pier became the property of the SIC, who themselves had been acquired by the Owners of the Middlesbrough Estates the previous year following the formation of a Local Board in 1880 to administer the town. Henry Pease, the founder of Saltburn-by-the-Sea, died the following year.

The new owners of the pier carried out a number of improvements to the structure during 1884. The pier head was widened and a bandstand was provided, complete with seating protected by glass screens. At the shore end of the pier, the entrance kiosks were replaced by two larger buildings, designed in matching style to those of the new incline tramway, which had replaced the dilapidated hoist. One of the kiosks was used as a café/pavilion and the other as ladies and gentlemen's cloakrooms. On 20 July 1887 the pier was illuminated for the first time by electric light.

During the later Victorian period and into the Edwardian, Saltburn blossomed into a popular resort for those who preferred to shy away from too many boisterous amusements. The pier provided genteel band concerts during the summer and bracing promenading, whilst on the sands, Little Tommy's Nigger Troupe, Mulvana's Minstrels and Grapho & Jackson's Mascots provided a variety mix of music, mirth and magic. The pier suffered from storm damage, but escaped relatively unharmed until 1924...when disaster struck.

On 7 May 1924, the china clay vessel *Ovenbeg* (formerly the Russian registered *St Nicholi*), carrying a cargo of china from Fowey to Grangemouth, was driven ashore by her captain just north-west of the pier during a strong gale. While out in the North Sea, the *Ovenbeg* had sprung a leak and was making for Hartlepool for repairs. However, while rounding Huntcliff, the pump broke down and the captain, who was part owner of the vessel, decided to bring her into Saltburn and beach her as she was rapidly filling up with water. The crew of four were rescued by the Saltburn Lifeboat.

The weather moderated during the day and it was hoped that the *Ovenbeg* could be re-floated. However the gale returned with a vengeance at nightfall and repeatedly forced the stricken ship against the pier until

A postcard view by Valentines of the pier taken from the pier head c.1900. Marlinova Collection

An Edwardian view of Saltburn Pier showing the enlarged entrance buildings erected in 1884. Marlinova Collection

The incline tramway from the pier in 1906. This had been opened in 1884 to replace the rather rickety hoist and is one of only three surviving water-balance cliff lifts in England. The lift station and pier entrance buildings were built in matching style. Marlinova Collection

A view of Saltburn Pier from the beach at low tide c.1910. Marlinova Collection

The SS *Ovenbeg* lies stranded by Saltburn Pier on 7 May 1924. Marlinova Collection

The *Ovenbeg* lies wrecked on the beach after crashing through Saltburn Pier on 8 May 1924. Marlinova Collection

Saltburn Pier Cut in two 8th May 1924.
A. E. Graham, Copyright, Redcar.

The gap in Saltburn Pier caused by the *Ovenbeg* collision, which was to remain in situ for six years. Marlinova Collection

Saltburn Pier in 1931 following the restoration of the breach caused by the *Ovenbeg*. The centre portion of the building at the pier entrance was added in 1929. Marlinova Collection

The Pier, Saltburn-by-Sea

The sad state of Saltburn Pier at the end of the Second World War. Beyond the shelter is the breach made in 1940 as a defence measure, while in the foreground the decking has all been stripped away. Marlinova Collection

it broke through the early hours of the following day, leaving a gap of 210ft. The guilty vessel was then washed ashore further down the beach, a mangled wreck. Local rumour maintained that a figure of a Russian monk had been seen walking the deck before the vessel foundered, as though giving warning of impending doom!

A barrier was erected at the end of the shortened pier, which enabled the remainder of the structure to still be used for promenading. In September 1924 Saltburn & Marske Urban District Council discussed purchasing the pier, pleasure gardens and cliff lift but decided against it. A private company's scheme to purchase the pier in 1925 also met with failure. On 30 March 1929 it was announced that the gap in the pier was to be repaired and a saloon added at the entrance to be used for dancing, concert shows and meetings. Steel was used in the reconstruction and in 1930 the full length of the pier was reopened.

In June 1938 the council finally acquired the pier at a cost of £12,000. However, two years later, 120ft of the steel section at the sea end was removed to prevent the pier being used by the enemy in the event of

Although restored by 1952, the pier suffered further damage during the infamous storm of 31 Jan/1 Feb 1953 which necessitated a further period of closure. This view of the pier and cliff lifts in the 1950s shows the pier deck closed and stripped of timber. *Marlinova Collection*

An almost deserted Saltburn Pier in the 1960s. Note how the centre building has been cut back to align with the two side buildings. *Marlinova Collection*

Saltburn Pier in 1974, unsafe and closed to the public due to the loss of some of the supporting piles during the previous year. Marlinova Collection

Saltburn Pier photographed during the storm of 29 October 1974, just moments after the collapse of the pier head into the sea. Courtesy of the late Norman Bainbridge

an invasion. The military also stripped the pier of its wooden decking, leaving it largely inaccessible.

By the end of the war, the pier was in a very poor condition having also suffered storm damage. On 18 August 1945 the council accepted a tender of £3,057 to repair the pier, although no work was carried out. The matter was brought before the council again on 6 September 1946 when they discussed *restoration of the pier, consequent upon partial destruction by the War Department and storm damage. Work has been met partly by the War Department and by the council's insurers, but further work is needed for the restoration of decking and bearer beams.*

On 5 April 1949, the Municipal Engineer for the council inspected the pier and found that the timber superstructure was in a very dilapidated condition. The 12 × 6in supports had rotten to at least half their depth and corrosive rotting had affected all points of fixation, and there were extreme lateral and vertical movement of the present structure, which could make it dangerous to the public walking on the beach or to coastal shipping. A planning application to repair the pier was granted on 13 April 1949 by the Ministry of Transport, Docks & Canal Division. However, due to the shortage of steel, work to reinstate the wartime gap was not commenced by the Skinningrove Iron & Steel Works until 1951.

Eventually at Easter 1952 the pier was reopened to the public and over 25,000 people used it during the first month. The official reopening took place on 31 May 1952. Unfortunately within a year the pier was closed again after gales had badly twisted the main structure, and it was to be another five years before it could be reopened after a further expenditure of £23,000.

Yet in spite of all these troubles, the pier remained a popular attraction throughout the 1960s and up to 90,000 people a year continued to frequent it. Fishing from the seaward end was the main source of income, though the café and amusement arcade were also profitable.

However, by the early 1970s the structure was once again giving cause for concern. In the autumn of 1971 one of the supporting piles on the seaward end was lost, and though it was replaced the following year a consultant engineer's report stated:

The general appearance of the pier is unfortunately marred by the extensive rusting of much of the steel and ironwork forming the main structure. However it has plenty of reserve strength, enabling it to stand safely when some members are heavily corroded or missing. It has in the past survived the loss of a pile with no apparent ill effect.

The damaged seaward end of Saltburn Pier following the loss of the pier head on 29 October 1974. The steel section of 1930 can be clearly distinguished from the original 1869 cast iron pier. Courtesy of the late Norman Bainbridge

Demolition of Saltburn Pier's 1930 steel section in 1976. Courtesy of the late Norman Bainbridge

A new pier head for Saltburn Pier 1977. Courtesy of the late Norman Bainbridge

Saltburn Pier reopened to the shorter length of 681ft in 1978. Marlinova Collection

Former Minister of Culture Chris Smith reopens Saltburn Pier on 13 July 2001 following restoration work at a cost of £1.8million. Courtesy of National Piers Society

A view looking along the Saltburn Pier from the pier head, June 2004. Marlinova Collection

An underwater survey confirmed that many of the supporting piles (especially the 1930 steel section) were in a poor condition, and in January 1973 the pier was declared unsafe to use, except in calm weather.

In June 1973, a pile was lost on the western side of the pier head and in the following November the loss of a further pile on the eastern side saw the pier closed altogether. Two months later the situation worsened when three further piles were lost in a storm. The Borough and County Councils drew up an interim plan to provide emergency repairs at a cost of £40,000, but before this could come into effect a severe storm on 29 October 1974 washed away the pier head and badly damaged the remainder of the pier, thus reducing its length to 1,100 feet.

By now Langbaurgh Borough Council (who had acquired the pier following the local government reorganisations of 1974) had decided enough was enough and in March 1975 they applied to the Department of Environment for permission to demolish the pier (this was necessary, as it was a listed building). An action group was formed by Langbaurgh councillor Audrey Collins, which forced a public inquiry to be held over three days in November 1975. As a result of the inquiry, the Secretary of State for the Environment, Peter Shore, granted listed building consent for the demolition of the thirteen end trestles only (comprising the steel section).

In September 1976, restoration work began with the demolition of the thirteen end trestles at a cost of £18,500. The remaining 681 feet of the pier was completely refurbished at a cost of £52,000 and on 29 June 1978 it was reopened to the public for the first time in nearly five years. In the following year the buildings at the pier entrance (which Langbaurgh Council had applied to demolish in May 1977) were restored. The cladding dating from the 1950s was removed and new cladding reflecting the original exposed timber framing was introduced in an attempt to restore the Victorian character of the pier. Internal subdivisions were removed to create a single open space and the building was let on a maintaining lease as an amusement arcade.

During the next twenty years the pier continued to provide in its own unassuming way an enjoyable promenade and amusement area for many visitors and locals. However the ever-forceful actions of the North Sea ensured that by the late 1990s further work was necessary on the structure. Following an initial rejection, a National Heritage Lottery award was granted in October 1999 and additional funding from the European Regional Development Fund, Redcar & Cleveland Borough

The Doughty Survivor

Council (who own the pier) and the Friends of Saltburn Pier allowed the £1.8 million reconstruction scheme to commence in May 2000. The main task was to refurbish the cast iron columns and re-secure them firmly into the seabed, and replace the steel deck beams with those of hardwood. The amusement arcade at the entrance to the pier was unaffected and remained open during the work. On 13 July 2001 former Minister for Culture, Chris Smith, reopened the pier and so commenced the latest chapter in the life of this lone survivor of the Yorkshire coast, a pier that simply refuses to die.

Saltburn Pier in May 2007. Both the pier and cliff lift are kept in good order by Redcar & Cleveland Council. Marlinova Collection

Chapter Four
The Battle of the Piers

Coatham Pier (1872–99) and Redcar Pier (1873–1981)

The twin coastal settlements of Redcar and Coatham were established by the de Brus family of Skelton soon after the Norman Conquest. Although Coatham has virtually lost its identity within an expanded Redcar, it was initially the more important village. For a time it was Cleveland's second most important port behind Yarm before the Tees Navigation Company was created by an Act of Parliament. Situated in the manor of Kirkleatham, the village also had a salt making business by boiling sea water. Redcar was part of the manor of Markse. In 1762 the manor was purchased by Sir Lawrence Dundas and in 1838 his grandson was created Earl of Zetland.

Redcar and Coatham's broad swathe of golden sands were first advertised for sea bathing in 1770 by Sir Charles Turner of Kirkleatham. He introduced bathing machines onto Coatham sands so that his own company, and the neighbourhood, might have the convenience of bathing without the trouble or expense of going to Scarborough.

In 1808, the villages were visited by a well-known historian named William Hutton, who wrote of his journey from Birmingham to Redcar and Coatham in his piece *Trip to Coatham*:

> After a journey of 184 miles, the last 25 of which were in the finest part of the road, though without a turnpike, we arrived at Coatham and Redcar, which although two villages, or rather hamlets, yet by their vicinity, I must consider as one. They are in the infancy of their existence, and I shall have the honour of being their first historian.
>
> Coatham is half a street, that is built only on one side, consists of about 70 houses and is 400 yards long. We then pass over an open green in the same line 400 yards more, which brings us to Redcar, which is one street on both sides, 500 yards, and containing about 160 houses. The green mentioned above will perhaps one day be built up, which is another reason for visiting Redcar and Coatham now.
>
> These two hamlets an age back could not have been no more than small fishing places....most of their old whitewashed houses have low buildings in front....and the two streets of Coatham and Redcar are covered with mountains of drift sand, blown by the north-west winds from the shore.

By 1810 Redcar had around a dozen bathing machines and in the succeeding thirty years appears to have stolen a march on its neighbour as a seaside watering place; according to W H Harrison's *Visitors Guide to Redcar* (1841):

> Formerly a very humble fishing village, consisting of but a few huts and hovels of miserable construction and appearance, inhabited by fishermen and their families; is pleasantly situated near the margin of the fine broad firm sands of the German Ocean, on the south-east side of the mouth of the River Tees, in the North Riding of Yorkshire, but by a steady and progressive improvement, it has now become a fashionable resort for sea bathing, and is much frequented in the summer months, by families of the first respectability, from the adjacent and distant counties. Harrison noted the attractions for visitors as numerous bathing machines, hot, vapour and other baths, 'Red Lion', 'White Swan' and 'Crown & Anchor' inns and broad, firm and smooth sands.

However, Harrison was not so enamoured of Coatham:

> At a short distance from Redcar, to the west, is East Coatham, in the parish of Kirkleatham; an ancient hamlet, containing one row of houses facing the sea, about quarter-a-mile long, belonging principally to the owner of the Kirkleatham Estate. Graves, in his history of Cleveland, says 'This was formerly a fishing town of some importance, and, with Redcar, contributed towards the supply of the neighbouring monasteries in this part of the county with fish. It is pleasantly situated a short distance from the shore, and was previous to the place, and contains some neat houses, well adapted for lodging houses. At that time there was a very extensive and commodious inn (now a farmhouse), which was greatly frequented by families, and having the advantage of firm and extensive sands, was the rival of Redcar, as a seat of seclusion for the invalid. The 'Lobster Inn' – the only one there at present – was formerly of great notoriety, and there are many of the then visitors at Coatham now living, who can relate the pleasures and enjoyments which they experienced on their annual visits to that place.'
>
> From the cessation of visitors to Coatham, in consequence of Redcar having so successfully taken the lead, the village seems to be much neglected, and a few individuals only, who cannot find accommodation in Redcar, or who prefer privacy and seclusion are to be found locating there during the bathing season. The bathing machines, formerly so much in use there, have vanished, and seemed to have joined their rivals at Redcar.
>
> It is to be regretted that Coatham has so much retrograded in utility and appearance, and from being equal, if not superior to Redcar, one would scarcely suppose at present, it had ever a claim to be so honourably noticed in Hutton's 'Trip to Coatham'. Yet, if the inhabitants would even now exert themselves, there is no doubt, but soon, it might partly resume its wonted

celebrity; and though, perhaps, not to equal, still it might vie with its rival neighbour.

Three years later, in 1844, Charles Dickens visited the area and left unimpressed, describing it as a 'long cell'.

The scars and shifting sandbanks off Redcar, coupled with shallow navigation channels at the mouth of the Tees, made this stretch of coast particularly treacherous for shipping and local fishermen. This led in 1802 to the establishment in Redcar of one of the earliest lifeboat stations in Britain. The station was furnished with a boat by pioneer lifeboat builder Henry Greathead of South Shields, which was later christened the *Zetland*. The craft survives as the oldest lifeboat in the world and can be viewed in the lifeboat museum on the seafront.

In 1846, the Stockton & Darlington Railway was opened to Redcar and visitor numbers began to increase. The impetus provided by the railway led to the landowners of Coatham, the Newcomen family, developing the village from 1860 as a select resort and Teeside commuter suburb. Good quality villa and terrace accommodation was provided and the seafront was enhanced with a new sea wall and promenade. In 1861, the Coatham Convalescent Home was opened at a cost of £4,500. The building could house fifty patients at a time (principally miners from County Durham recovering from sicknesses) and was staffed by volunteers and the Sisters of the House of the Good Samaritan. The Coatham Hotel was opened in 1870, although its original planned size was never completed.

Coatham took on a superior air to Redcar, which was much resented in the latter. Although largely owned by Lord Zetland, Redcar also had a fair number of smaller freeholders and its development was less uniform than its neighbour. The growth of the Cleveland iron trade led to Redcar housing a large proportion of working class people employed in the industry. The town also had a small fishing fleet.

The *Watering Places of Cleveland* (1869) described Redcar as:

the best known of the watering places of Cleveland, and although it cannot boast of being as fashionable as some of the other localities on the north-east coast, still it is every year the resort to which many hundreds of health or pleasure seekers find their way.

The main attraction, however, of Redcar is the sands, which are considered to be the most extensive in the kingdom, running from Saltburn-by-the-Sea to the Tees bay, a distance of seven or eight miles, and are of unrivalled firmness and purity. The formation of the beach is admirably adapted for sea bathing, being of a very gradual slope, whilst several lines of rock hidden at high water and stretching far out to sea, serve to break the violence of the waves.

> To the west of Redcar stands Coatham. These two places were formerly separated from each other by green fields, but now they adjoin, and are in fact one town.

Many outsiders did indeed consider Redcar and Coatham as one town, but for now Coatham fiercely protected its own identity. When the proposal for a pier for the area was mooted in the 1860s, it would have made sense for a joint pier for both towns. After all, their combined population in 1871 was only around 3,500, and visitor numbers at Whitsun for that year was less than 5,000.

On 2 August 1866, the Redcar Pier Company was registered by Joseph Emmerson Dowson of 4 Victoria Street, Westminster, London. Dowson was a noted pier contractor who had worked with Eugenius Birch on some of his piers. An Act of Parliament for authorisation to construct the pier was gained four days later. However, there was a distinct lack of support in Redcar for the pier, including from Lord Zetland, and only seven shares were taken up, all held by the nominees of the company.[3]

The Redcar Pier scheme lay dormant until a pier for Coatham was proposed in 1870. James Rutherford, the agent for the Newcomen Estate had announced plans to build the select Coatham Victoria Hotel and the prospectus for the hotel stated that *a company for the erection of a promenade pier immediately in front of the hotel is in contemplation.* On 22 September 1870 the Coatham Victoria Pier Company was registered with the Board of Trade. Two sites were considered for the pier: one opposite the Coatham Hotel, the other at the end of Lobster Road. Many of the hotel's shareholders also took shares in the pier company and this encouraged Rutherford to reject any thoughts of combining with the Redcar Pier Company. He expressed his thoughts in the *Middlesbrough Evening Gazette,* using the signature 'S.P.', on 26 October 1870. He stated that *the proposal to make a pier at Coatham has aroused the dormant energies of its* (Redcar's) *public men and the long unheard of pier at Redcar is to be constructed forthwith. Let not the public be in haste to take the bait.* Three days later Rutherford argued that a pier serving both resorts should be placed at Coatham, *which is used by more refined and fashionable visitors. The pier would be well away from the bathing beach at Redcar used by thousands of excursionists who visit for sea air and an annual wash.*

Negotiations recommenced between the Redcar Pier Company and engineers J E & A Dowson. A board meeting of the company was held on 21 October 1870 and they expressed confidence that the Coatham team would soon join them. On 28 October the *Redcar and Saltburn Gazette* commented:

Engravings of Coatham and Redcar piers shortly after they were open to the public in 1872–3. Marlinova Collection

An opinion has been mooted, which we deem it necessary to notice, that the movement (for building Redcar Pier) is got up in "opposition" to Coatham. That this is contrary to facts is easily shown, for the Act of Parliament for the "Construction, Maintenance, and Regulation of a pier at Redcar, in the County of York", was in existence years before the Coatham scheme was thought of, and would have been carried out long before this, had not the want of public spirit in the place delayed the design of the first promoters in a way that is almost unaccountable, except to those who know how difficult it is to move Redcar to action, even on points intimately connected with its own interests. Doubtless the proposal for a pier at Coatham has aroused the inhabitants of Redcar to the consciousness of their possession of an Act of Parliament, which may at any moment be carried out, provided that the amount necessary for the erection can be obtained.

It is also contended that Coatham presents a better site than Redcar can for the erection of the pier, and at this moment it is certainly worthy of consideration whether such is the fact or not. What, then, are the particulars of the selection of the Redcar site? Briefly these: in 1864, the late M.E. (sic) Dowson Esq of London, and his friends, surveyed the coast, and decided on the bay opposite Redcar for these reasons, viz, that a pier could be constructed here at considerably less cost than at any other point; that deep water could be reached so that steamers might at low tide touch and land passengers; and that there would be shelter afforded at the pier-head in bad weather by the surrounding rocks, which form a natural breakwater; the latter also being the reason why Redcar was recommended by Sir Henry Hope, when on the Harbour Commission, as a place especially adapted for the construction of a Harbour of Refuge, there being in fact already a natural basis for a harbour, only requiring the art and constructive skill of the engineer to complete what nature had begun. The decision of Mr Dowson and his friends was afterwards fully endorsed by Euguene (sic) Birch Esq, the eminent engineer, who visited Redcar in 1868, and after full inspection of the proposed site, recommended the east end of Redcar as the point especially favoured by nature for the erection of a pier; it having at once the advantages of deep water for landing, and of moderate cost of construction, in consequence of the superior height of the cliff for an approach, and the short distance to High Stone, the place indicated as a spot for the pier-head. It is therefore: perfectly clear that the site for Redcar Pier was selected with an especial view to suitability; and not to please the inhabitants of Redcar, who might feel flattered by the selection of the bay opposite, although it would have entirely otherwise had the natural formation of the coast been different.

With respect to the proposed pier at Coatham, a very long pier would be needed before deep water could be reached, and then the very exposed condition of the coast west and north-west of West Scar is such that whenever there is a slight gale no vessel dare approach the rocks, in consequence of the dangerous swell which prevails.

With regard to any opposition or jealousy between Redcar and Coatham, on this or any other subject, all thinking minds must be agreed on the utter absurdity of any such feeling, as the interest of each place is interwoven with that of the other; and whatever tends to increase the attraction of either as a watering place undoubtedly benefits the other directly or indirectly, by bringing to the seaside yearly an increasing number of visitors, upon which the ultimate prosperity of both depends.

On 3 November 1870 a meeting was held between the Coatham and Redcar pier companies. Coatham stated that they were erecting their pier at the end of Newcomen Street, a site central to the resorts and close to the Redcar boundary, and hoped their neighbours would join their scheme. The offer was rebutted however, and the Redcar Pier Company resolved to construct their pier at the end of Clarendon Street (moving it from the original site at King Street), far eastward from the Coatham site.

The two companies therefore went ahead with their separate proposals, in spite of the ominous warning forewarning of the *Redcar & Saltburn Gazette* of 4 November 1870:

It is obvious to all that one pier, well constructed, and with sufficient depth of water at the pier-head, would amply satisfy the wants of the whole population – visitors and inhabitants – of both Redcar and Coatham. Nay, more, the very smallness of the population forbids the supposition that two piers will pay.

The same edition of the paper reported on the formation of a pier company for Coatham:

THE PROPOSED PIER AT COATHAM. A meeting of the promoters of the new promenade pier at Coatham was held at the Lobster Hotel, on Friday last, when it was unanimously decided to proceed with the formation of a company for the purpose of carrying the same into execution forthwith. The sum of £3,000 was subscribed, and further promises made will considerably increase this amount. The capital is to be £7,000, the engineers being John Fowler C.E. Stockton (Engineer to the Tees Conservancy Commission), and Charles John Adams, Coatham and Stockton.

The 'Northern Echo' of the 1st inst contains the following paragraph: 'we have it on good authority that the eminent architect, Mr J.C. Adams, and Mr Fowler C.E. are in treaty for castings for the Coatham Pier, with an extensive firm in Middlesbrough. Our informant states that an influential gentleman from Stockton is negotiating the proper arrangements with the Board of Trade for commencing the work forthwith.

The exposed nature of the Coatham Pier site was of concern to one of its residents:

To the Editor of the Redcar and Saltburn Gazette. SIR – As a resident in Coatham, and personally interested in the prosperity of the place, I would be glad to be informed how far the proposed pier to be erected at the end of Newcomen Terrace may be considered in the light of a safe investment, and whether the site selected by the engineers of the promoters is positively a safe and proper site in respect to the security of the structure from the special violence of the waves at this point of the coast, and the safety of the pier-head as a landing place for vessels. The latter part of this enquiry I think is of special importance, seeing that the landing – if really such can be secured at that place – must be at the seaward side of the rocky ledge which abuts the shore. I would also be glad to know whether a pier has ever been erected where the conditions of coast are similar to those which exist at Coatham. Until I am positively informed by a reliable authority of the eligibility of the Coatham site, I must hold my own opinion; that the pier constructed there will be specially liable to accident by sea currents, and be totally unfitted as a safe landing place for vessels. Yours truly, Q.

On 11 November 1870, the Coatham Victoria Pier Company, registered at the Old Hall, Kirkleatham, was incorporated by the Coatham Pier Order for a

pier, jetty or landing place at East Coatham in the Parish of Kirkleatham, in the North Riding of York, commencing from and near Newcomen Promenade at a point opposite or near to the northern end of Newcomen Street and extending thence seawards for a distance of 750 yards or thereabouts to a point beyond the rocks called West Scar Rocks, roads, approaches, landing stages and other conveniences connected there with the embarking and landing of passengers, fish, goods and merchandise, and other purposes, and also to erect, construct, alter, and maintain, upon or in connection with the said pier, jetty or landing place, toll-houses, shops, saloons, bazaars and other buildings, and to construct alter and maintain a floating and other baths and landing stages to be placed in the sea wall adjacent to the said pier, jetty or landing stage, and to conduct and manage, let or sell the tolls, toll-houses, shops, saloons, bazaar, baths and landing stages, or any of them, when so constructed.

The chairman of the Coatham Victoria Pier Company was Arthur Henry Turner Newcomen of Kirkleatham Hall, who held 200 shares. £5,500 had been subscribed and on 23 December 1870 the Pier Order was presented to the Board of Trade. The proposed rates for customers using the pier were: ship passengers 6d, promenaders 3d, bath and sedan chairs 6d, perambulators 2d, vessels 10s, trunks 2d–8d (depending on weight), baths – warm 3s, shower 2s 6d, cold 2s, reading room 6s.

However, there was opposition to the Coatham Pier from the local fishermen and boat pilots, and on 29 November 1870 they petitioned the Board of Trade:

> If the pier is erected in a north-easterly direction across the Rock called the West Scar, according to the present plans, it will not only seriously injure, impede and obstruct us in our said occupation, but will also greatly endanger our lives and property, and in case of any vessel striking on the West Scar, which frequently happens in storms, that it will be impossible to launch the lifeboat by her being dashed against the stanchions of the said pier erected across the West Scar; and moreover that the danger of all vessels off the coast in stormy weather will be greatly increased by the erection of such pier across the West Scar. And we further represent to your Honourable Board that a Provisional Order has already been granted for the erection of a promenade pier at Redcar, at a point where it will be neither dangerous nor injurious to ourselves and to others, and within half mile of the site of the proposed pier at Coatham and that the proposed pier at Redcar will be amply sufficient for the requirements of the inhabitants and visitors to both Coatham and Redcar, which two villages adjoin one and other. We therefore humbly pray that your Honourable Board will not grant a Provisional Order for the erection of any promenade pier at Coatham and more especially that you will not allow such pier to be erected in a north-easterly direction across the West Scar to the injury and danger of ourselves and others being in vessels off the coast in stormy weather.
>
> 41 fishermen and pilots

A further petition against Coatham Pier, signed by forty-three Redcar pilots and fishermen, was presented to the Board of Trade in January 1871. In response, Rutherford (who was also secretary of the Coatham Victoria Pier Company) organised a counter petition signed by 22 local mariners, along with others from the Teeside area, the Chief Officer of the Coatham Coastguard and the Inspector of Lifeboats, who claimed that that the pier would not be detrimental to navigation or the lifeboat service. This was received by the Board of Trade on 25 January.

Six days later, the first annual meeting of the Coatham Victoria Pier Company was held at the Lobster Hotel, when it was announced that the whole of the Company's capital had been subscribed.

During the following month the Redcar Pier Company announced their prospectus and share capital, which was £10,000, divided into 1,000 shares of £10 each. The directors were headed by Rear-Admiral Chaloner, and the Company Secretary was J H Webster. The engineers were Messrs J E & A Dowson of 9 Great Queen Street, Westminster. The prospectus stated:

The Company was formed in 1866, for the purpose of providing Redcar with a commodious Promenade and Landing Pier, and in that year the construction of the works was authorised by a Provisional Order obtained from the Board of Trade and confirmed by 'The Piers and Harbour Orders Confirmation Act 1866.'

The Company, having decided to alter the site of the pier, have since made application to the Board of Trade for a Provisional Order for the amendment of 'The Redcar Pier Order 1866', which when granted, will enable them to construct the pier in a situation in every respect the most eligible.

It affords the Company the greatest satisfaction to be able to state that The Right Honourable The Earl of Zetland, K.T., as Lord of the Manor of Markse, in Cleveland, has given his entire consent to the undertaking, and that His Lordship has most handsomely promised to subscribe £1,000.

The pier, which will command charming views of the Bay of the Tees and the Yorkshire coast, will commence at or near a point on the sea wall, now called 'The Esplanade', nearly opposite to Clarendon Street, in Redcar, extending from such point into the sea of distance of 1,300 feet, or thereabouts, in an East North Easterly direction; and at the pier head there will be suitable landing accommodation, and a sufficient depth of water to enable passengers with ease and safety to embark in and disembark from steamers and pleasure boats at any state of the tide.

Besides the fact (which indeed is of paramount importance) that the site selected possesses a naturally formed and always accessible sheltered deep water channel for steamers, and is undoubtedly the best in an engineering point of view that can be obtained, it has other great advantages, which must at once be obvious.

Amongst others may be mentioned its proximity (without being objectionably near) to the boating and bathing, which are such great attractions on the far-famed sands of Redcar and the ready access which visitors (and especially excursionists, who always frequent Redcar beach) will have to the shops, hotels and other places for refreshment.

As a fashionable watering place, Redcar – which has the good fortune to be situate in the Cleveland district, where the iron trade is being so wonderfully developed, and in the midst of a vast and ever-increasing community – has for many years been the favourite resort of visitors; no only from the neighbouring towns of Middlesbrough, Stockton and Darlington, but also from many large and populous places at a greater distance: and, commensurate with its rapidly increasing importance and necessities, during the last few years many new houses and buildings have been erected, and together with other considerable improvements, the sea wall, which is about 850 yards long and has a carriage way sixty feet wide, has been constructed, at a cost of nearly £2,000.

Eligible building land, with sea frontages, lies at the East End of Redcar, and there can be no doubt that the extension of the town, which has already been commenced in that direction, must soon be continued.

The pier, which will be constructed on iron piles, will be both substantial and ornamental, and at the pier-head, a capacious and elegant reading room, or saloon, and refreshment rooms, with every convenience, will be erected; whilst care will be taken to provide proper seat accommodation wherever it may be needed.

The company have full powers to prevent any person from shipping fish or anything which in their judgment might in any manner interfere with the use of the pier for recreation, or for the embarking or landing of passengers, and care will be taken that such powers shall at all times be properly exercised [the landing of fish had been a part of the company's original plans for the pier, but had been dropped following disapproval from the Board of Trade. Such trade would have been at odds with the usage of the pier as a fashionable promenade].

The designs have been prepared, with due regard to economy, by engineers who are well acquainted with and are well known in connection with structures of this kind, and it is fully anticipated that the whole of the works will not cost more than £6,000.

The great success of pier companies generally and the high dividends paid by them where much larger sums have been expended, fully justify the belief that the Redcar Pier – economically but substantially constructed; and efficiently managed – cannot fail to be a source of considerable profit to investors.

A large portion of the capital has already been subscribed.

Despite claiming a preference for the Coatham site, the Board of Trade granted both pier orders as they were unwilling to countenance objections arising out of *opposition between local interests*. Nevertheless, they added that there was *no necessity for two promenade piers within 800 yards of each other*. Their preference for the Coatham site at Newcomen Street was based on the fact it was close to Redcar railway station (300 yards away at the other end of the street).Coatham also had a higher population; of 2,200 in 425 houses, plus a grammar school, Friends Meeting House, Wesleyan chapel and school and a convalescent home (with chapel). Redcar on the other hand had a population of just 1,300 in 270 houses. The Board also viewed that the Coatham Victoria Pier Company consisted of *gentlemen, most of whom are well-known in the locality and are deeply interested in its progress and development, who have subscribed the whole of the £10,000 required.* They considered the objection to Coatham Pier from the fishermen was not capable of being sustained.

The Battle of the Piers

The *Redcar and Saltburn News* of 17 March 1871 commented:

> The 'Battle of the Piers' is at an end – for the present at least – and the result is, each party holds its own ground, neither is vanquished, perhaps neither can claim victory, though each may say the other has sustained a defeat.

During May 1871, the Bills for both piers were published. The proposed length of Coatham Pier was 2,250 feet, and it was to have toll-houses, shops and a reading and refreshment saloon. Initially, both pier companies petitioned against their rival, although Redcar withdrew theirs. Coatham's objection led to the Bills being referred to a Select Committee of the House of Commons. This was heard on 2 June 1871 and the Committee passed both pier bills.

Redcar was the first off the mark with the driving in of its first pile, by Rear-Admiral Chaloner, on 28 August 1871. The *Redcar and Saltburn Gazette* recorded the event and also gave details of the pier's engineering:

> DRIVING IN OF THE FIRST PILE – Monday, the 28th inst, was a day of high rejoicing at Redcar, in honour of the commencement of Redcar Pier. The first pile of which was driven by Rear-Admiral Chaloner in the presence of the directors, shareholders, engineers, contractors, and a large concourse of people, including visitors and inhabitants of Redcar and the district. The weather was propitious, and the proceedings of the day were of the heartiest character, and were characterised by the most complete success.
>
> The site chosen for the pier is Clarendon Street nearly opposite the church. In fact nearly at the east end of the town, and was indicated by a display of bunting. The pier will run east north east, and will be 1,300 feet long and 20 feet broad. The head of the pier will be widened out to an area 114 feet long by 65 feet broad, and a separate landing stage is to be placed beyond the head for the landing of passengers from steamers and cobles. The piles are of cast iron, 9 inches in diameter, sharply pointed at the end, and will be driven by a heavy pile driving machine into the rock. To these piles will be attached columns placed in pairs 30 feet apart, and battering inwards. Additional stability will be given to these columns by a strong wrought iron bracing, and on top of the columns will be ornamental cast iron spandrills stretching between each pair of columns. These spandrills will be connected transversely by flooring joists of timber, on which the planking of the pier will be fixed. A handrail of wrought iron will run along each side of the pier, and at intervals seats will be placed for the accommodation of visitors. The upper railings of the palisade will carry the gas to eighteen lamps of a very beautiful design. The engineers for the pier are Messrs J.E. & A. Dowson, Great Queen Street, Westminster,

London, the contractors being Messrs Head, Wrightson, and Co. of Stockton-on-Tees, and, from what is known of both the engineers and the contractors, we feel convinced that the pier will not only prove an ornament to Redcar, but will also prove a first-class piece of workmanship.

A procession marched from the company offices in the High Street to the site of the pier where a pile driver had been erected. Making up the procession were *the police, the Redcar & Coatham Band, Directors, Engineers and Contractors to the Company, Rear-Admiral Chaloner, Rev. W. Milburn, shareholders, inhabitants and visitors.*

Following speeches by J H Webster, the Company Secretary, and Rear-Admiral Chaloner, the Rev W Milburn offered up an appropriate prayer before the Admiral drove in the first pile. The procession then marched to the Royal Hotel where a luncheon was laid on.

The construction of Coatham Pier was also soon put in hand. On 8 September 1871, it was announced that Messrs Hopkins, Gilkes & Co. had been appointed contractors *who expect to be well forward with the work by the beginning of the next season.* The conveyance of the Coatham Pier site opposite Newcomen Street was formally acknowledged by the Board of Trade on 28 October.

During a meeting at the Lobster Hotel called on 17 November by the promoters of the Coatham Pier scheme, John Fowler revealed that it was cheaper to fasten the piles onto the rocks rather than in deep water, and the end of the pier would be in ten feet of water at low tide.

In its editorial of 18 November 1871 the *Redcar & Saltburn Gazette* revealed where its pier sympathies lay:

All hope of amalgamation of the two pier schemes has entirely vanished and it will now be well to look steadily at the hard facts of the case, some of which are very hard indeed. Much obloquy has been cast upon the people of Redcar, and torrents of unmitigated and unmerited censure have been showered on our devoted heads, doubtless with the express intention of putting poor old Redcar under water, to make room for her wealthy and prosperous neighbour Coatham. We will not pause to remark on the spirit which has dictated such an attempt to write down Redcar as we have recently witnessed, believing as we do that error will ultimately and necessarily fall to the ground before the superior claims of truth. But we will proceed to examine the question raised by the opponents of the Redcar Pier which we deem absolutely necessary to be examined in the interests of justice and truth. And it must be borne in mind that during the whole of this exciting controversy we have consistently maintained the principle that the interests of Redcar and Coatham are identical; that together they form in the minds of visitors (their chief supporters) one united whole; and it is only on the spot that the diverse spirit prevails to such an extent as to mar the good feeling which ought ever to exist in a community seeking to live by the suffrages of supporters from without. The point, then, which we propose to examine, is the relative selfishness or disinterestedness of the two promoting parties.

It has been broadly stated that the Redcar people are determined to have the pier built where it will especially benefit adjacent property, as if this were not emphatically the principal if not the sole reason for promoting a pier at Coatham. It is quite patent to all that the erection of a pier will enhance the value of property in its vicinity, and the Redcar people are not insensible to this obvious advantage. But had there been no other reason for promoting a pier at Redcar than the mere improvement of property, the question would never have been mooted. The primary reason for proposing the construction of a pier at Redcar was its especial suitability for such an erection. It is needless to go over the grounds which have been stated again and again why Redcar was selected by engineers having no connection with it as the place 'par excellence' pointed out by nature for a promenade and landing pier. Be it remembered, however, that this was the sole primary reason why Redcar was selected, which would not have been the case at all without the natural advantages alluded to.

But what is the principal reason why a pier is desired at Coatham? Is it because there are remarkable natural facilities existing? Or that philanthropy suggests that the erection of a pier would relieve the dullness of the shore skirted by the West Scar? It is certainly not the former, if we concede a shadow of fact to the latter. But this latter consideration alone hardly accounts for the strong influences which are at work to make the pier at Coatham 'un fait accompli'. The publication of the prospectus throws considerable light on the subject, for we find the same potent and influential names in the directory of the proposed Coatham Victoria Pier as appear in the directory of the Victoria Hotel. It would appear, therefore, that the interests of the two schemes are identical, and that the reason for building a pier at Coatham is purely speculative and commercial. No we don't find fault with the promoters of these undertakings, for all successful commercial enterprises tend incidentally to promote the prosperity of their vicinage; and that it may be hoped that the hotel at Coatham will be no exception; on the contrary, we wish it a hearty success. But what we do find fault with is the systematic attempt to bolster up the notion that Coatham is in every respect a naturally superior place to Redcar for building a pier, when the contrary has been completely demonstrated. The case may be fairly stated that Redcar has certain natural advantages for a pier, advantages so great indeed that safe and permanent structure could be erected at a comparatively small cost; whilst Coatham has certain natural disadvantages in consequence of which the cost of construction would be double of that Redcar, even supposing a pier could be successfully constructed at West Scar Head, which is held by many observant persons to be next door to an impossibility.

We are glad to hear that the Redcar Pier promoters, undaunted by the difficulties which have been unexpectedly arisen, are determined to proceed energetically with their project, which we hope will be carried out successfully, and prove a source of pleasure and convenience to visitors, a safe and profitable 'investment to the shareholders and an ornament to the place'.

Work on both piers proceeded through the winter of 1871–2. At a meeting of the Redcar Pier Company on 4 April 1872 it was reported that £1,660 had been received in shares up to the end of 1871, although not all of the shares had been subscribed. £983 1s 1d of the money had been accounted for, whilst £678 2s 2d was in hand. By May 1872, 800 feet of the 1,300 feet Redcar Pier had been built, whilst Coatham Pier was advancing rapidly with 1,700 of its 2,250 feet completed. The platform for the pier's reading room and music saloon was already erected, as was a considerable portion of the handrail. The brick entrance lodges had been commenced and it was intended to open a section of the pier to the public in the middle of June.

The partially built Coatham Pier was in fact open to the public for the first time on 4 July 1872 *with a considerable display of bunting*. The pier's opening hours were 9am to 10pm, and Groening's band performed on Tuesdays and Thursdays at 11–1 and 6.45-8.45.

Unfortunately, in a portent of what was to come, the *Redcar and Saltburn Gazette* on Friday, 17 July 1872 reported:

Accident at Coatham Pier – on Wednesday last, an accident of a very serious nature occurred to the Coatham Pier. The men were engaged in boring on the rocks until it was too late to get up the outrigger (the apparatus by which the piles are driven). The result was that at high water the sea dashing it with great violence swept it away. The damage done cannot at present be estimated, but it must be very serious as well as causing a delay of several weeks. Fortunately none of the workmen were engaged at this part of the pier at the time of the accident.

There was further storm havoc on 21/22 September 1872, this time to both piers:

During the prevalence of a storm from the north-east which raged here with great violence on Saturday and Sunday last, the stage and apparatus used for fixing the piles of Redcar Pier was washed away. Fortunately it fell clear of the piles, or the damage might have been serious; but when the sea settles sufficiently it will be recovered. The outrigger, which is used for fixing the piles on the Coatham Pier, was also washed away; but it was eventually recovered.

The Coatham Hotel was opened opposite the pier on 12 October 1872, and by the end of the year Coatham Pier had taken £207 5s 3d in tolls. The pier would not be fully completed until the summer of 1874, but on 14 February 1873 it was reported that *Redcar Pier is nearing completion; the length of the pier and one side of the pier head is complete.* The last pile was fixed on 7 March and in the following month the windscreens on the pier head were in the course of erection.

The date for the official opening of Redcar Pier was set for Whit Monday, 2 June 1873, although one of its principal supporters, the Earl of Zetland, had passed away on 6 May. The pier was officially opened by Mrs Dawson of Weston Hall, who deputised for the indisposed Rear-Admiral Chaloner. A public procession left the registered office of the pier company in the High Street at 11.45, arriving at the pier head for noon where the opening ceremony took place. Both Redcar lifeboats were manned and afloat and in a display of 'pier solidarity' Coatham Pier was bedecked with flags. Following the opening ceremony, a public luncheon was held at the Royal Hotel where J H Webster, the secretary of the Redcar Pier Company, toasted the success of both piers in the presence of James Rutherford, his counterpart at Coatham Pier.

The final cost of Redcar Pier was £9,785 (construction £9,221, engineering £563). The 1,300ft structure was of a particularly elegant design which made good use of high quality castings in its main members. The 20ft wide planking deck, on 8in × 3in joists at 3ft centres, was supported on cantilever cast iron arch beams/girders. These cantilevered girders spanned 30ft with a total depth of 5ft at the column supports, and 12ft at mid-span. The columns had conical solid cast iron capitals in Egyptian style, which connected the cantilever arch girders to the columns. These columns stood on cast iron bases not less than 1¼in thick, which were fixed to the underlying shale rock. The columns were tied by 1½in diameter wrought iron cross bracing. The pier had a widened approach supported by cast iron lattice girders connecting six main columns to the stone retaining wall of the promenade. The pier's appearance was enhanced by the addition of three distinctive minaret kiosks at the entrance housing the toll office and ladies and gentlemen's cloak rooms. The pier head was 114ft wide and housed a bandstand complete with sheltered seating for 700 people.

Sadly, engineering details for Coatham Pier are far less exhaustive. The pier was a cast iron structure of 2,250ft in length, the longer distance being necessary to reach the deep water at this point of the coast. Landing steps and a small stage were provided for boat traffic. A glass-fronted saloon, which was also used as a reading room and refreshment house was erected on a stage fixed onto the north side of the pier just over halfway along its length. The entrance to the pier consisted of two octagonal-shaped brick buildings: one used as a toll house, the other as a small newspaper and book shop. A metal sign bearing the legend PIER was erected across the entrance between the two kiosks.

The 1873 summer season for the two piers got under way on Tuesday, 17 June when a band was engaged to play on Coatham Pier. On the following Saturday, Mr T. MacLagan provided entertainment in the saloon at 8.30 in the evening. F Groening's Military Band (who had played on Coatham Pier the previous summer) began their engagement on Redcar Pier on Tuesday, 24 June. During July, the Coatham Victoria Pier Saloon presented Miss Lydia Howard *the wonderfully gifted little fairy actress, elocutionist and singer of eight years of age, who appears in her marvellous musical and dramatic entertainment, assisted by Mr A. Stirling & Miss K. Power; Music Director, Mr Alexander Murray. Performances on July 10–12, 14–16, reserved seats 1s, to commence 8.30 p.m., tickets at Mr Bates' Library and at the pier entrance and saloon.* In deference to its supposed status as the superior resort of the two, an orchestral band was also engaged to perform in the Coatham Pier Saloon.

During August 1873 the entertainment on Redcar Pier consisted of the Redcar & Coatham Band on Mondays, Wednesdays, Thursdays and Saturdays between 7–9 p.m. and Mr Groening's Military Band at other times, admission prices 2d–3d. On 6 August the pier held a Grand Fete Day where Mrs Dawson inaugurated the use of the temporary landing stage and presented two silver cups for a boat race from the pier. She also provided the cost of the band. During the Redcar Regatta on 21 August, the Redcar & Coatham Band played on the pier.

Mrs Dawson was again present on the pier on 18 October during a race held between Redcar and Staithes fishermen from Coatham to Saltburn piers. The Redcar boys won the £200 prize and a large crowd gathered on Redcar Pier to witness Mrs Dawson present the four winning fishermen with a bottle of champagne and a sovereign.

Both piers enjoyed a moderate first full season. Coatham took £373 12s 6d in tolls, but this was offset by the cost of the orchestral band, which was £124 5s 0d. At Whitsuntide 1874 Coatham Pier attracted 1,830 visitors on the Monday as opposed to Redcar's 616. On the following day the total was Coatham 1,000, Redcar 600. Coatham was proving to be the more popular of the two piers, although its initial aspirations of attracting just a select clientele had to be tempered with the realism that it was the excursionists who would make the pier pay. Nevertheless, they were only coming to the two resorts in limited numbers, and because of the duplication of facilities, prices had to be kept low. However this discouraged the more discerning visitor, who wished not to rub shoulders with the trippers on the piers.

As the summer season approached, the *Redcar & Saltburn Gazette* commented in its 29 May 1874 issue:

> The two piers add greatly to the attraction of the place. The Redcar Pier, which was completed last year, is ready for landing passengers by steamers. The Coatham Pier is rapidly approaching completion, and is also ready for steamboat traffic. The Directors of the Redcar Pier Company have engaged Mr Groening's fine military band, which gave so much pleasure to both visitors and inhabitants during last summer. The band performances will commence the last week in June. Lets hope that the weather is maybe more propitious than last year, when the band nights were often a failure through rainy weather.

The same newspaper also had to report a sadder event:

> Joseph Carter of Redcar fell off a plank under Coatham Pier on Wednesday, 27th and drowned. He worked on the pier as a labourer and left a widow and three children. A subscription list has been started.

Groening's concerts on Redcar Pier were advertised from 26 June:

> REDCAR PIER – MR F.GROENINGS GRAND MILITARY BAND performs on this pier. EVERY MON, WED & FRI during the season. Afternoon performance 3–5 3d, Evening performance 6.45–8.45 4d, military band of 16 performers' conductor Mr Franz Groening. Vocal quartets in the evening by Messrs S. Norton, Jos. Fawcett, S. Rogers & J. Fawcett. Programmes to be had at the entrance to the pier, one penny.

On 10 July a sea trip was advertised from Redcar Pier:

> The fast sailing 'Storm King' will leave Redcar Pier tomorrow at 10.30 for Saltburn, returning at one. At three in the afternoon the same day 'Storm King' will leave the pier for a trip to sea.

Coatham Pier continued to provide its genteel entertainment. During July Bruce & Verne gave their 'Drawing Room Entertainment' in the Coatham Pier Saloon to *small but thoroughly appreciative audiences, who frequently testified their application by healthy outbursts of applause.* There was also a promenade concert by J Imerson of Middlesbrough to raise funds for the lifeboat and convalescent home.

The generous Mrs Dawson continued to fund some of the attractions on Redcar Pier. On 1 August she headed a 'select party' at the regatta *which dispensed mirth and champagne with lavish kindness.* She also paid for a firework display on the pier six days later. The final band concerts on the pier were held on 25 September.

However, the 1874 season once again saw the two piers achieve only moderate success. The tolls collected on Coatham Pier were slightly down on the previous year, amounting to £366 12s 11d. Unfortunately, matters for the pier were about to take a serious turn, as vividly described by the *Redcar & Saltburn Gazette* on 11 December 1874:

Terrific gale on North East Coast – five ships wrecked at Redcar – Coatham Pier rent into three parts: The heavy gale which swept over the United Kingdom was felt with especial severity on the North East Coast. No storm of such violence having visited this coast since the well-known Whitsuntide storm of 1860, when twelve sailing vessels and one steamer were wrecked between the Tees and Saltburn. The storm arose about midnight on Tuesday, and raged with terrific violence till Wednesday morning. Many people in Redcar, beside the fishermen, were aroused about four o'clock, and witnessed the scene on the beach. Thomas Picknett was the first to raise the alarm, he was up late, or rather being early attending to the safety of his boats, when he saw a vessel drifting over Saltscar Rocks, and he at once called the attention of the coastguard on watch thereto. After which he proceeded to rouse the fishermen by beating the 'tattoo' on the lifeboat drum. In attempting to launch the new lifeboat the combined action of the wind and surf stove in the boat, and she could not be used. The new lifeboat was taken out because it was nearer the scene of the distress than the old boat, and fishermen were willing to give it a fair trial. It has had this, and at least in this instance was a failure. Although the weather was squally on Tuesday, and gave indications of the impending gale, it was not until a late hour that the wind veered round to the north east, and caused the sea to roll in; breaking over the Redcar, Coatham and Saltburn piers. The wind, which blew in fitful gusts, was accompanied by rain and sleet, and the weather at midnight was of the most wretched description. The drifting vessel proved to be the brig 'Garibaldi' of Cowes, 196 tons, which was driven over Saltscar and stranded near Coatham Pier. The captain and crew were saved by the rocket apparatus under the command of Mr Bates, Chief Officer of the Coastguard. The vessel was disabled but otherwise injured. The gale continued to increase and between two and three o'clock, when the gale was at its height, the brig 'Griffin', of Southampton,

The *Griffin* lies stranded on the beach after breaking through the shore end of Coatham Pier on 9 December 1874. A further breach beyond the pier saloon was made by the *Corrymbus*. The pier had only just been completed to its full length of 2,250ft. Marlinova Collection

under Master Mundy with a crew of seven, bound for Sunderland, came direct on to the Coatham Pier. She appears to have been laden with elm, part of which had been discharged at various ports, and shortly before midnight they shortened the sails in consequence of the storm. They shortly afterwards appeared to lose all knowledge of their position; the wind and rain almost making it impossible to see any distance before them. Between three and four o'clock the vessel, as just stated, came right on to the Coatham Pier. The master and crew, who had given themselves up for lost, and had taken to the rigging, leaped onto the pier as the vessel went through, and all escaped uninjured, with exception of the master, who had one of his hands somewhat severely hurt. The 'Griffin', in passing through the pier, carried away several yards of the deck and spandrills of the pier, and knocked down several rows of piles. The figurehead, bowsprit and bulwarks of the vessel were much damaged. After striking and getting clear of the piles, she drifted about 100 yards in shore, and became stuck fast in the sands nearly opposite the Coatham Hotel. It was subsequently found on the tide receding, that the bulwark at the stern had been broken and had sustained other damage of a lighter character. The master and crew, on reaching the shore, were taken to the Cleveland Hotel, Coatham. The 'Corrymbus', a Dundee schooner of 91 tons sailing from

Boulogne to Shields with master Alexander Petrie and five hands, also ran through the pier from the north side almost immediately afterwards. The pier took away her bowsprit and her bulwarks are likewise damaged, but the hull is intact and made no water. The crew remained on board until the tide receded and then came ashore. This vessel drifted a few hundred yards west of Coatham.

Redcar on Wednesday and yesterday was visited by a large number of persons from Middlesbrough and Stockton, who having heard of the destruction wrought by the gale, went down to gratify their curiosity. Upon arriving at Redcar, a most appalling spectacle presented itself to their view, the ships strewn about the coast and the Coatham Pier having been cut into three pieces – two vessels having cut right through the pier. Near to the entrance to the pier, large heaps of wreck was piled, and numbers of persons were on the beach. A continual stream of persons visited the pier and walked along it as far as was deemed safe. The gap made in the pier nearest the land shows that about six lengths of the pier have been taken away. The other break in the pier is one that was made by the schooner passing through and taking about four or five lengths away. It is estimated that the damage will be from £1,000–1,500.

Mr Hoggard of Grant Villa, Coatham, with his accustomed business tact, has taken a large photograph of Coatham Pier in its broken condition, with the brig 'Griffin' in the foreground. Handsomely-mounted copies may be had at the office of this paper, price 5s.

Westwards from Redcar are the remains of Coatham Pier, plans, cordage etc.

Locals who gathered to watch the mountainous seas reported that the waves washed right over the deck of the two piers. In all, some thirty vessels came ashore on the Cleveland coast during the storm, while at Whitby ten vessels came ashore or were wrecked, with the loss of a master from one vessel, a cabin boy from another and the crew from a small 'Billy Boy' craft. The South Shields barque *Henry Cooke* was lost with all her eighteen hands outside her home port. A total of thirty seamen were lost during the night.

The Coatham Victoria Pier Company responded to the disaster by increasing their share capital by £6,000 (1,200 shares of £5 each). On 19th February 1875, the repair of the pier was let to Mr Hunter of Middlesbrough, with Messrs Aiken & Co responsible for the casting of the piles. Two months later it was reported:

The repairing of Coatham Pier is being pushed rapidly forward; the gap nearest the shore will soon disappear. It is probable that the broken portion

An early view of Redcar Pier which shows the short-lived landing stage at the pier head. Marlinova Collection

north of the saloon will take considerably more time to repair, on account of the difficulties presented by that portion of West Scar Rock, on which the pier is built.

Over the Whitsun holiday both piers were said to be 'extensively patronised'; the inner breach having been repaired on Coatham Pier. On 28 May the *Redcar & Saltburn Gazette* reported improvements to Redcar Pier:

We understand that the Directors of Redcar Pier will once again retain the services of Mr Groening's fine band, which was so great an attraction last season. They have also made a great improvement at the pier head, by removing the bandstand to the entrance of the windscreens, by which the whole space inside the screens will be available for promenading. It is further intended to make the landing stage more perfect by lengthening the existing wooden piles, which by the experience of last summer were found to be insufficient at high tide.

On 27 August J S Levett exhibited his patent safety life float and swimming aid on the pier, which attracted 780 visitors at a cost of 6d each (sadly, Levett was drowned in Blackpool on 7 August 1876).

August 1875 also saw the case of Coatham Victoria Pier Company v Alexander, owner of the *Griffin*, came before York Assizes. The pier company claimed negligence and wished to recover £620 in damages, whilst Alexander stated that he saw no lights on the pier. The case was referred to the higher court.

On 21 October 1875, Redcar Pier was damaged during a violent gale on the north east coast, which saw the sea rise to a tremendous height. A wooden girder, with pieces of ironwork attached to it from the wrecked Saltburn Pier, struck the east side of the pier, snapping off one of the iron columns, and afterwards getting entangled with the column opposite the one broken, against which it struck with every wave. Efforts were made to remove the wreckage by means of grappling irons and ropes, as it was feared still greater damage would be done, however this was not achieved until the tide had abated.

The damage to the pier was repaired over the winter and in January 1876 it was reported that Coatham Pier had been fully restored to its full 2,250ft. A new fixed light had been placed on the pier head and the pier was now lit by gas.

The half-yearly meeting of the Redcar Pier Company in March reported a balance of income over expenditure of £256 10s. However, liabilities remained on the capital account of £335 19s 11d.

The 1876 summer season on both piers began in earnest in June at Whitsuntide. On Coatham Pier Tom Walker displayed Captain Boynton's life-saving apparatus, but only to a limited interest. Franz Groening's Band was once again the feature on Redcar Pier from 26 June. Afternoon performances were given on Mondays, Wednesdays and Saturdays from 3-5p.m., admission 3d, although excursionists showing a railway ticket were charged only a penny. Evening performances were held from 7.30-9.30, admission 4d. During August the Band of Otley Engineer Volunteers gave two grand promenade concerts on the pier.

Coatham Pier's big summer attraction was a new skating rink which was opened adjoining the entrance on Saturday, 5 August 1876. Roller skating had become very fashionable and the Coatham Victoria Pier Company had high hopes that the rink would go some way to finally making the pier profitable.

Sadly, these hopes were to be quickly dashed when winter storms once again wreaked havoc on the pier. During a gale on Tuesday, 31 October 1876 waves were reported to be breaking right over the pier. The structure largely escaped damage on this occasion, but it was not to be so fortunate two months later, as reported in the *Redcar & Saltburn Gazette* on Friday, 22 December:

One of the very few photographs showing a close-up view of the intact Coatham Pier, probably taken c.1890. The roller skating rink, added in 1876, can be seen and the left hand entrance kiosk is boarded up and out of use. Marlinova Collection

Terrific Gale – Coatham Pier Head and lighthouse washed away – Damage to Redcar Pier. Since an early hour of Wednesday morning a terrific storm has been raging on the north-east coast and Coatham Pier has again suffered extensive damage. In the great storm of 9th December 1874 two vessels were completely driven through the pier in separate places, the brig 'Griffin', the remains of which still lie on the beach opposite the Coatham Hotel, carrying away about sixty yards between the entrance to the pier and the saloon, and the schooner 'Corrymbus' making a gap of 40–50 yards wide near the extreme end of the pier. The damage, which amounted to about £1,500, was not fully made good until last autumn, when the whole of the pier was again thrown open. Much more serious is the present disaster, as over 200 yards at the pier head is washed away. This occurred yesterday morning, when the storm was at its height, and immense seas broke heavily over the structure. The head of the pier was of course much wider than the promenade, the massive timbers consequently offering greater resistance to the advancing tide, and at daybreak it was found that the whole of the upper part of the pier head, including the landing stage, and the lighthouse added in April last, had entirely disappeared. The part of the promenade which has come to grief includes the whole of that portion which was destroyed by the 'Corrymbus' already referred to, and which was last repaired. At the very lowest estimate the damage will amount to £3,000, and will probably exceed this sum. During yesterday the pier was visited by large numbers of persons, but the portion wrecked appears to have been completely carried away, and there is nothing to be seen from the deck save a solitary single pile, the column fitting into which has been lifted out as neatly as though the bolts have been unscrewed and the column taken out of the socket. It may be added that the portion of the pier remaining – about three-quarters of the original length – does not seem to be at all damaged, so that this will still be available for promenading purposes. The sands west of the Coatham Convalescent Home are thickly strewn with debris from the pier. Redcar Pier also sustained slight damage, part of one of the girders at the north-west corner, next to the landing stage, has broken off. Considering the violence of the storm, it seems incredible the structure has come off so well.

The storm had washed away 480ft of the sea end of Coatham Pier, leaving 1,770ft remaining. This time it was decided not to rebuild the lost section: the landing stage/steps having rarely been used as the West Scar Rocks had made it too difficult for boats to call. On 31 March 1877 the Coatham Victoria Pier Company reincorporated the company as the Coatham Pier Company and the old company, which had last met on 11 September 1875, was put into liquidation. The new company announced a share capital of £10,000 (1,000 × £10 shares).

Nevertheless, the sad, slow decline of Coatham Pier had begun, with the company seemingly losing their enthusiasm for their seemingly ill-fated structure. The forewarnings that the two piers could not pay due to the limited visitor numbers was proving to be true, and Coatham, originally the more popular of the two piers, was now losing out to its rival. The concerts and entertainments in the Coatham Pier Saloon apparently dried up (they were certainly not advertised) and it became a haven of quiet contemplation. The craze for roller skating soon passed (although it returned with a vengeance in 1908) and it's unclear how long 'rinking' remained a feature of the Coatham Pier rink.

Henry Barraclough directed the band on Redcar Pier for the 1877 season, although the Otley Engineers Volunteer Band once again returned in August.

The following year saw Barraclough return to Redcar Pier, along with the North Durham Militia Band. At Whitsun 2,100 people visited the pier, but otherwise daily attendances could be pretty mediocre and the Redcar Pier Company were unable to pay a dividend to shareholders as the £164 8s 6d in credit was used to pay off debts. On 15 April 1878 the share capital of the Coatham Pier Company was altered to 2,000 × £5 shares from £1,000 × £10. During the same year the registered office of the company was moved from the Kirkleatham Estate Offices in Redcar Road to the one of the entrance lodges of the pier.

The year 1879 proved to be an uneventful one for the two piers. The Redcar Pier Company reported that it was not a prosperous year for them, although the balance was on the 'right side'.

The band fare for the 1880 season remained pretty much unchanged. The North Durham Regiment of Militia opened the summer season in June and it was completed by the North York Volunteer Band in August. The October weather of that year proved to be very stormy and on Thursday, 28, a terrific gale blew up from the east-north-east. The Sunderland schooner *Luna* was almost blown into Coatham Pier before she was driven ashore close to the Warrenby Steelworks. Her crew of four were rescued by the lifeboat *Emma*. A further vessel, also called the *Luna*, was travelling from Rochester to Shields under the command of Captain Friend when she was driven helplessly before the storm and became stuck on East Scar. However, shortly before 1.30am the following morning the *Luna* was driven off the rocks and was carried through Redcar Pier, leaving a breach of 180ft after five of the supporting columns were carried away. The unfortunate Captain Friend suffered a broken leg after one of the columns passed through the cabin skylight. The *Luna* came to rest just north of the pier and the situation for her crew of seven looked grim with both the Redcar lifeboats *Burton-on-Trent* and *Emma* put out of action. Furthermore, the rocket brigade had used up their allocation of rockets. Nevertheless, the Redcar fishermen decided to launch the famous old lifeboat *Zetland* (which had been retired some ten years earlier) and she safely brought the crew of the *Luna* to safety. However the vessel was a total wreck and was sold off for scrap.

The gap in the pier was repaired by Head Wrightson in time for the 1881 season. However, the following year saw the death of Mrs Dawson, a generous supporter of Redcar Pier.

There was not such charitable support for Coatham Pier. By 31 December 1882 only 730 of the 2,000 shares in the Coatham Pier Company had been taken up. At an Extraordinary General Meeting of the company in March 1883, it was agreed that 900 of the £5 shares should be converted to preference shares; the holders being entitled to a fixed cumulative preferential dividend at the rate of five per cent per annum for the time being paid upon such shares (paid half-yearly 1 September and 1 March). 150 shares of the preference shares were taken up by the directors of the company: namely Messrs A Newcomen, C Newcomen, Dodds, Jaques, Bolckow and Thompson.

The winter of 1882-3 was to bring further woe on the Coatham Pier Company. During the night of 11/12 December the skating rink abutting the pier entrance was blown down and the sands around were covered with wooden boards and skates. Redcar Pier also lost its landing stage during this period; apparently it was demolished by the SS *Cochrane*; although there is very little evidence that any ships called at the pier except during the first few years. In March 1889, a section of the pier gave way, and repairs had to be carried out by Head Wrightson.

The band performances on Redcar Pier at this time came in for criticism for their similarity each season. Military bands were often the usual fare: during the 1885 season for example it was the 4th Battalion of the Durham Light Infantry. On 3 August 1889, the *Redcar & Saltburn News* received the following letter:

> Why is Saltburn Pier cheaper than Redcar? The band plays there regularly and the company can afford to let the charge be three pence per head. Cannot Redcar people engage a string band – a local one – twice or thrice a week to play on the Redcar Pier, and occasionally the promenade? A bandstand could be easily moved along the promenade.

The letter must have had some effect, for in April 1890 a Public Band was formed by subscription. Arrangements were sought with both piers for the band to perform on, although, in the end, only Redcar was used. The leader of the band was Chas Lax of Hull and the performances began on 6 July for ten weeks. The band performed at various venues around the town, and on Redcar Pier on Sunday afternoons and Wednesday and Friday evenings. Admission to the performances was 3d; whilst admission to the pier was 1d and a fishing ticket was 4d. Around 700 people paid for admission to the first concert on the pier, although there was criticism that *the leader of the band might infuse more life into it and shorten the intervals*. There was also a report on *the sea trip on Thursday was a success and appeared to draw many visitors. A landing stage is sorely needed and would add considerably to the revenue of the pier company.*

The Redcar Pier Company's precarious finances meant that a new landing stage was off the agenda, although in 1892 the pier was repainted. That season however was not a successful one. Coatham Pier was fairing even worse and the Coatham Pier Company was pretty much out on its feet due to mounting debts. For the 1895 season Mr Bosomworth (an ex-policeman) was appointed Pier Master of Coatham Pier in place of Captain Croft.

Visitor numbers at Whitsun in 1896 were disappointing:

> The number of visitors who paid for admission to Redcar Pier on Monday and Tuesday were very small compared with previous years and the directors will have to provide something more attractive if they intend to keep pace with their competitors at Coatham.

The bandstand and sheltered seating on Redcar Pier 1895. They were destroyed by fire three years later in 1898. Courtesy of Kirkleatham Old Hall Museum

Redcar Pier Head from the beach at low tide c.1896. This view highlights the pier's graceful ironwork and the soon-to-be-lost bandstand and sheltered seating (upon which two men can be seen). Courtesy of Richard Riding

The wreck of the *Amarant* by Redcar Pier on 12 January 1897. The hull of the vessel was later re-floated and smashed its way through the pier, causing a breach of 300ft.
Marlinova Collection

The 'competitors at Coatham' provided the Cleveland Quartette Party and a Militia Band. On 17 July 1,000 people paid to go on Coatham Pier and listen to the Redcar Town Band and a group of Australian bell ringers. By this time however, the winding-up of the Coatham Pier Company had been announced, and their final meeting was held on 31 August.

The crashing of the Coatham Pier Company and concern over the condition of the pier led to its closure by the Newcomen Estate in 1897. That year also began disastrously for Redcar Pier, as reported in the *Redcar & Saltburn Gazette* on 23 January:

> The storm – considerable damage to property in Redcar has been done by the storm now raging. The brigantine 'Amarant', which came ashore last week, has been completely smashed up by the violence of the sea, which in turn has carried away about 100 yards of Redcar Pier.

The vessel had been noticed drifting between Coatham and Redcar with its boarding lights burning, yet no one was found aboard and it appears that it had been abandoned in thick fog. The *Amarant* came ashore at Redcar but was further damaged in a storm and only the hull remained following salvage by locals. This was left on the beach; however, it became re-floated on the tide and smashed into Redcar Pier.

The Redcar Pier Company were unable to pay for repairs, and on 6 March 1897 the *Redcar & Saltburn Gazette* reported:

> An Extraordinary General Meeting of the shareholders of the Redcar Pier Company has been called for Tuesday, 9th March for the purpose of considering the best means of restoring the damaged condition of the pier caused by a vessel having been driven through it during the last storm, whereby it sustained damages estimated at £1,100. The directors have been endeavouring to raise funds for the necessary repairs by mortgage, but have failed to do so. The shareholders will have to decide whether they will subscribe for debentures of preference shares. Failing any decision being arrived at, a resolution proposing that the company be wound up voluntary will be brought forward.

Fortunately a £1,000 mortgage was offered to the company by two local gentlemen at 6% interest. Head Wrightson carried out the repairs at a cost of £1,075 and on 1 July 1897 the pier was reopened with a concert by Les Pierrots, which was watched by 500 people.

The Hemming Company opened the 1898 season on Redcar Pier whilst Coatham Pier remained closed. Regrettably disaster struck Redcar Pier again during the night of 12 August 1898 when the pier head was destroyed by fire. The blaze was fought by the Redcar and Kirkleatham fire brigades, but due to their hose pipes not being long enough to reach the fire decking had to be ripped up to prevent the flames spreading along the pier. It is believed that the fire was started by a lighted wax vesta that had fallen between the planks. The shattered pier head was cordoned off and the rest of the pier remained in use for promenading and fishing.

The next disaster to strike Coatham Pier however finally signalled the end of the pier. On 18 October 1898, the Finnish barque *Birger*, bound from Carlos in Spain to Abo in Finland with a crew of fifteen went through the pier during a storm. The boat had been sighted at 9.30am by the Scarborough Coastguard flying signals of distress, but before the lifeboat could be launched the *Birger* had been driven helplessly northwards. The rocket brigade continued to track the hapless ship by road for eight miles before they turned back. The *Birger* narrowly avoided hitting Saltburn Pier, in the process narrowly outstripping the Saltburn Lifeboat, before striking the Saltscar Rocks off Redcar with such force that the fore and mizzen masts came crashing down, killing

The final end of Coatham Pier's sad life came when the *Birger* went through the pier on 22 October 1898. Marlinova Collection

the master and a mate. The RNLI lifeboat *Brothers* was launched, as was the old lifeboat *Emma* by a volunteer crew of fifteen. However the latter vessel was in a poor condition and three of the oars snapped off as it was rowed into the sea. The craft was then left at the mercy of the waves and was swept underneath Coatham Pier before being deposited on the beach. By this time several thousand spectators from both Coatham and Redcar had gathered on the promenade to witness the *Birger* breaking up in heavy seas, sweeping all but three of its crew into the sea. They managed to cling onto a piece of wreckage and as they passed under Coatham Pier ropes were lowered to haul them to safety. One of the men managed to scramble onto the pier, but another sadly fell back into the sea to his death. The third man was washed up on the beach unconscious where he was revived and taken to the Coatham Hotel. Those people who had gathered on Coatham Pier to witness this sad spectacle then had to run for their lives as the wrecked *Birger* came towards the pier. Eventually it crashed through the structure close to the saloon, causing a 300ft breach, before coming to rest on the beach. The two surviving crewmen, John Malika and Emil Nordstrom, were sent to the seaman's mission house at Middlesbrough. The deceased crew were laid to rest at Seaton Carew.

An elegantly attired Victorian lady poses in front of the isolated saloon of Coatham
Pier during the demolition of the structure in 1899. Marlinova Collection

As Coatham Pier lay fatefully broken, a proposal to sell Redcar Pier in November 1898 was rejected by the company's shareholders. In the following month, the *Redcar & Saltburn Gazette* reported:

Redcar Pier – At the adjourned meeting of the shareholders held at Redcar yesterday, Surgeon-Col Locke, Chairman, presiding; it was decided to pay off half the present mortgage and restore a portion of the pier head, comprising ironwork and decking, and leaving sufficient space for a bandstand and promenade around it for use next season.

The restoration however was not fully completed until 1901.

The sad fate of Coatham Pier was revealed by the *Redcar & Saltburn Gazette* on 25 February 1899:

Coatham Pier, which has had a very chequered and disastrous career, is to be sold by auction and to be dismantled. The sale will be conducted by Mr Henry Hudson, auctioneer, under the instructions of Mr G.T.O. Newcomen. The pier was built about 30 years ago and cost £17,000. Five years later (sic) it was cut into three parts during a heavy gale by vessels dashing against it. A little later during another storm, the end of the pier for a fourth of its length was washed away, and the pier company went into liquidation. It was at that time estimated to be worth £6,000. Recently it has come into the hands of Mr Newcomen, and last autumn was completely cut in two by the ill-fated 'Birger'. It had long been condemned by the authorities as unsafe.

The sale of the pier took place at the Lobster Hotel on Thursday, 27 April, which was reported on by the *Redcar & Saltburn Gazette* two days later:

Coatham Pier sale – A large assembly of gentlemen assembled at the Lobster Hotel on Wednesday last (sic), when the Coatham Pier was offered for sale by public auction. The pier was erected 27 years ago by a company of local gentlemen at a cost of £17,000, but it proved an unfortunate structure, being frequently damaged by storms, and it never paid a dividend. At length it became part of the Kirkleatham Estate, and since 1897, owing to its dilapidation, it was closed to the public as being unsafe, whilst last October it was cut in two by the wreckage of the 'Birger', creating a considerable gap in its length between the shore and pavilion. This sealed its fate, and it was offered for sale; the purchasers to remove the material within six months from date of sale. The portion offered extends from the skating rink seawards, about 355 yards (1,065ft) of thereabouts and including the concert saloon with all its interior fittings complete, as well as the metal columns, wrought iron girders, tie rods and handrail stays, and the timbering is of pitch pine and best redwood. The

The entrance to Redcar Pier c.1904 featured on a postcard by Brittain & Wright, Stockton-on-Tees. The kiosk fronting the promenade is housing a small shop, and a selection of amusement and sweetmeat machines can also be seen. Marlinova Collection

An Edwardian postcard of Redcar Pier in the Reliable Series c.1905. The three ladies in the foreground may have been superimposed! Marlinova Collection

sale attracted considerable public attention. The auctioneer described the stipulation as to removal, and stated that there were 100 columns and the same number of straight iron girders, 350 lengths of pitch pine joists measuring 20ft × 12in × 4½in thick, as well as the decking, the saloon etc. During the past three years, the estate had spent £200 in timbering alone. Bidding started at £100, and was quickly followed by offers up to £390, when the auctioneer declared an open sale. After further completion with Mr George Morrison of Borough Road East, Middlesbrough, the property at length was knocked down for £400 to Mr J.H. Sellars, representing Messrs Ellison, Cordingley & Co, Spen Valley Works, Cleckheaton.

The dismantling of the seaward end of the pier began almost immediately, with the glass saloon left in splendid isolation for a time. The wreck of the *Birger*, which was drifting dangerously close to Redcar Pier, was also finally secured. The shoreward end of the pier, which appears not to have been included in the auction, remained in situ for a while longer. The skating rink, which was situated adjoining the pier entrance but was not on the structure itself, also eventually disappeared, leaving just the entrance kiosks as a reminder of an ill-fated venture.

The demise of its pier in 1899 finally signalled the end of Coatham's aspirations as an independent resort, and in that year it merged with Redcar to form Redcar Urban District Council.

Meanwhile, Redcar Pier held a series of charitable concerts during September 1899. However, during a storm two months later, part of the decking was torn up.

As Redcar entered the twentieth century, a small portable bandstand trundled along the promenade between Redcar and Coatham giving alternate band concerts. This was replaced by a permanent bandstand erected on the promenade in 1905 at a cost of £400. A semi-circular shelter with seating and public toilets was added in 1910 at a cost of £1,000.

A small bandstand was also placed on Redcar Pier in 1901, along with sheltered seating following the reconstruction of the fire-damaged pier head. The Eston Steelworks Silver Band performed on the pier at Whitsun that year and Ben Bedford's Orchestral Band were engaged twice daily from 21 July, in conjunction with variety entertainments. These included Mappin & Johnson's Royal Pierrots with afternoon performances and Mr Hugget's Band in September. Fishing was also an attraction on the pier: *Redcar & Saltburn News* 5 January 1901:

> Lovers of fishing note that there have been some large fish recently caught off Redcar Pier. Since Coatham Pier was removed Redcar Pier has become the favourite resort of fishers and they are generally well rewarded for their efforts.

The surviving entrance kiosks of Coatham Pier c.1907. The temporary building by the kiosks was used for pierrot shows. Marlinova Collection

A postcard of Redcar Pier in 1909 featuring the new pavilion that was added that year. Marlinova Collection

Redcar Pier c.1912 after a slight extension in the size of the pavilion. Marlinova Collection

The Cosy Corner or 'Glass House' erected for concert party shows at the entrance to the former Coatham Pier in 1910. Note the pier kiosks incorporated into the building. Marlinova Collection

Redcar Pier in 1922 showing a further extension of the pavilion. Marlinova Collection

A busy scene on Redcar Pier Head photographed during the 1920s. The buildings were erected in 1902 to replace those destroyed in 1898 by fire. Courtesy of Redcar Library

The Redcar Pier Company's half-yearly report in March 1901 reported a balance-in-hand of £197 8s 1d, the best figures yet, enabling contracts to be put out for painting the pier and repairing woodwork. £484 14s 4d had been received in revenue, of which £42 0s 9d was for fishing tickets, £8 17s 5d for use of lavatories and £8 17s 4d for the automatic machines. In all, 80,000 people passed through the pier's turnstiles in 1901 in what was a record year for visitors to the resort.

The rise in popularity of Redcar as a resort escalated during the Edwardian era as trippers descended on the town from Middlesbrough and County Durham. The promenade was extended and widened and a new bandstand was added, whilst on the beach were refreshment kiosks, a steam roundabout, helter skelter and other amusements. Other attractions included parks and the racecourse. Pierrots such as Johnny Groves Royal Redcar Pierrots performed on the sands and the pier and also at the entrance kiosks to the vanished Coatham Pier. Sam Paul's Cleveland Cadets in their naval style uniforms were also popular in 1910-14 and Bert Leighton & His Redcar Follies performed on their alfresco pavilion on the beach.

Although the sceptics who had said back in 1870 that two piers would never pay had been proved correct, the one surviving pier was reaping the benefits of Redcar's new popularity and in 1907 it was announced that a pavilion was to be added to the pier. Work commenced in January 1909 and the landward end of the pier was widened to accommodate the pavilion, with new piles being added in line with the existing ones at 30ft intervals. A £1,000 mortgage had been secured from Thomas Phillipson to fund the work (which was paid off in December 1915). The pavilion was opened in May 1909 and six months later it gained a theatre licence. Pierrot shows, concert parties, plays and dances were held there, as was roller skating during the winter. In 1912 the pavilion was slightly enlarged to include a café.

At the old Coatham Pier site, a report in the *Cleveland Standard* on 2 January 1909 described it as *dilapidated and a disgrace to the town*. However, work began that year to incorporate the two surviving entrance kiosks into a new glass concert building, known as the 'Cosy Corner' or 'Glasshouse'. The Cosy Corner Pierrots, led by Jimmy Lynton, became a feature of the building during the 1920s before Lynton joined Billy Sorrow's Optimists, who also performed at the Cosy Corner.

In 1927 the Redcar Pier Pavilion was extended to the Esplanade at a cost of £3,129, although £93 was reclaimed from the purchase of the pier forecourt by the corporation and the sale of sundry materials. The pavilion was licensed for the showing of films and theatrical entertainments. Meetings were also held there; such as in June 1933 when it housed

The extension of the Pier Pavilion to the esplanade in 1928 is clearly seen on this postcard published by J Salmon in the 1930s. Sadly, this meant the loss of the distinctive minaret kiosks. Marlinova Collection

The New Pavilion Theatre and Cinema opened at the entrance to the old Coatham Pier in 1938. Marlinova Collection

150 delegates of the National Farriers & Blacksmiths Association. The distinctive minaret kiosks at the pier entrance were sadly lost when the pavilion was extended. The old kiosks of Coatham Pier also disappeared when the Cosy Corner was reconstructed as the New Pavilion in 1928. This in turn was re-styled as the Regent Cinema in 1964.

The interwar years saw Redcar at its zenith as a seaside resort. In 1923 Redcar Corporation acquired the foreshore rights from the Marquess of Zetland and vigorously promoted the resort as 'Redcar for Happy Holidays'. The extensive sandy beach was popular for sandcastle competitions, donkeys and Punch and Judy, while at Sunshine Corner Uncle Tom and his band of helpers sang songs (principally of a religious overture) and encouraged the family audience to sing along and perform their own songs on the stage, for which they were rewarded with a stick of rock. Other attractions included the Pleasure Park (with the Giant Racer rollercoaster), swimming pool at the Coatham Enclosure, Zetland Park, Palace Cinema and the Sea Car, a half boat/car that ran along the beach into the sea.

During the 1930s Redcar Borough Council expressed an interest in purchasing the pier, but negotiations with the Redcar Pier Company broke down in 1934. The council had wanted a reduction in the purchase price as £1,500 worth of repairs needed to be carried out to the deck structure. Four years later, the pier was again offered to the council, for £12,000, plus an additional £1,000 in compensation to the directors and officials of the company. Once again the council refused the offer.

Like its neighbour at Saltburn, Redcar Pier was breached in June 1940 as a defence measure. As the war progressed the isolated pier head was washed away by storms and the remainder of the pier was seriously weakened by an exploding mine, leaving it in a very poor condition. The council were still probing about buying the structure, and on 20 May 1944 it was reported:

> Redcar used to have two piers, now it has three-quarters of one and the future of that is obscure as the corporation have turned down a suggestion by the Pier Company to develop the shoreward end, and have asked the company what price they want for what remains of the entire structure.

It was stated that the company desired to extend the pavilion by 35 feet on each side to provide for a café and glass enclosed shelters with a promenade around them, leading to the promenade deck proper when reconstructed. The new pavilion would also be used as a dance hall and for musical entertainments, and it was intended to apply for an intoxicating liquor license. The proposals were made with a view to

Redcar Pier Pavilion in the 1950s, with dancing being prominently advertised. The much shortened pier ended just out of shot. Marlinova Collection

An interior view of the pavilion on Redcar Pier. Marlinova Collection

Dancing to Danny Mitchell and His Orchestra was a feature of the Pier Ballroom for a number of years. This view of the orchestra was taken in 1962 and features the £3,000 Hammond organ. Marlinova Collection

developing the shore end of the pier *to raise sufficient money to carry out the reconstruction of the seaward portion, and until that time the seaward pier promenade proper would be closed as it was in an unsafe condition.*

The council rejected the scheme as they stated they wanted the pier to be reconstructed as a whole. However, upon finally buying the pier for £2,000 on 18 May 1946, the council then stated that full reconstruction of the pier was not viable. They estimated that it would cost £1,000–3,000 to remove the pier wreckage from the sea and a further £1,000 to remove

The remaining stub of Redcar Pier left high and dry in 1975. Marlinova Collection

The frontage of the Pier Ballroom and Café in the 1970s. Marlinova Collection

the pier structure beyond the pavilion. Meanwhile, the winding-up of the Redcar Pier Company was confirmed on 2 October 1946. The final winding-up meeting of the company was held on 3 October 1947.

Between 1947 and 1950 the majority of the pier was demolished, leaving just the pier pavilion and a 45ft stub of neck beyond it. The pavilion was widened by 20ft on both sides and a new entrance was provided with shops and a café at a cost of £1,800. The pier was officially reopened at Whitsun 1947.

In January 1952, the Pier Ballroom (as it was now termed) was granted a bar licence. In addition to its function as an entertainment and dance hall, meetings were also held there. On 10 October 1952, over 1,000 people packed the ballroom to hear a speech by Dr Charles Hill, Parliamentary Secretary to the Minister of Food.

During the great East Coast Floods of 31 January/1 February 1953, the pier's supporting legs suffered damage. Repairs were carried out and the Pier Ballroom continued to provide entertainment for locals and visitors alike. Danny Mitchell and his Orchestra, featuring a £3,000 Hammond Organ, was a popular feature for a number of years.

Nevertheless by the 1970s, Redcar was in decline as a day trip resort and what remained of the pier was showing its age. In January 1976 the Pier Ballroom had to be closed after huge waves damaged the floor, and in April 1978 the council announced that £38,000 was needed for the repainting and repair of the pier's cast iron and steel support structure. In February 1980 they took the decision that the pier would close in November following the end of the Cleveland Organ Society's programme using the Wurlitzer Organ installed in 1978. The ballroom was duly closed and the organ was transferred to the James Finegan Hall at Eston. The pier was sold for demolition for £250 and by March 1981 the work had been completed.

The victor of the 'Battle of the Piers', Redcar, has totally vanished, save for a lump of concrete with the remains of a cast iron support, that has been placed on the beach to mark its site. Ironically there is a more permanent reminder of the long-vanquished Coatham Pier in the Regent Cinema that still fronts the entrance to the old pier.

The demolition of Redcar Pier and Pavilion was undertaken between December 1980 and March 1981. Marlinova Collection

The Regent Cinema on the site of Coatham Pier 1988. Courtesy of Daphne Leach

The anchor of the *Birger*, the vessel that wrecked Coatham Pier in 1898, on display on the esplanade at Redcar. Marlinova Collection

A piece of iron support embedded in a lump of concrete marks the site of Redcar Pier May 2007. Marlinova Collection

CHAPTER FIVE

A MAGNETIC ATTRACTION
FOR SHIPS

WITHERNSEA PIER, 1877-1903

Withernsea dates back to the reign of Edward the Confessor (1042–66), but the original village was washed away in 1444, a fate later suffered by the adjoining settlement of Owthorne during the nineteenth century. Withernsea was rebuilt and the commencement of a new church, St Nicholas, began in 1488. Coastal erosion however remained a serious problem in the area and one of the aims of Anthony Bannister in his creation of a seaside resort at Withernsea was a sea wall to halt the erosion.

Anthony Bannister, the founding father of Victorian Withernsea. Marlinova Collection

Alderman Anthony Bannister was a merchant and ship owner from Hull, who was the town's mayor in 1852. He was instrumental in opening the Hull and Withernsea railway in 1854 and engaged the renowned architect Cuthbert Brodrick[4] to design the Queens Hotel. Rows of elegant portico houses facing the sea were also planned by Brodrick but only two were built.

In 1862 the Withernsea line became part of the North Eastern Railway and increasing numbers of visitors, mainly from Hull, travelled to the resort. Bannister now drew up plans for the improvement of the town and formed the Withernsea Pier, Promenade, Gas & General Improvement Company (WPPG&GI), which was incorporated on 15 November 1870, with a capital of £40,000 (8000 × £5 shares). The company was registered at 17 Bowley Lane, Hull, and in addition to the provision of coastal defences, roads, housing and public services such as drainage and gas, a pier was also planned.

The pier was to be sited opposite Young Street and was to be *1,200ft long, on iron piles, projecting into the sea 380ft below low water mark, and from which passengers can embark and disembark at all states of the tide. The cost of erection of the pier complete in every respect is estimated not to exceed £8,000.* In addition to its function as a promenade pier, the landing of fish was also expected to be a profitable sideline.

By 4 March 1871, 350 shares had been taken up in the WPPG&GI, and in the following year a Provisional Order for the pier was granted by the Board of Trade. However no work was carried out and by 1874 the pier site had been moved closer to the railway station.

On 5 September 1874 the *Withernsea Chronicle* reported:

THE NEW PIER – we see by an advertisement, that offers of tenders are invited for the construction of an iron pier, for the Withernsea Improvement Company (Provisional Order granted).

One month later, on 3 October, the same paper stated:

WITHERNSEA PIER – This pier, for which tenders have been solicited, is now in a fair way of being pushed with vigour, the situation has been altered from

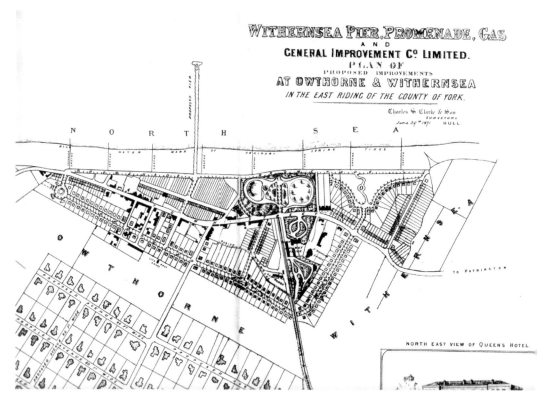

A map of the proposed development drawn up by the Withernsea Pier, Promenade, Gas & General Improvement Company in 1871. The site of the proposed pier was soon moved to opposite the railway station. Marlinova Collection

The Withernsea Pier, Promenade, Gas, and General Improvement Company, Limited.

Capital £40,000, in 8,000 Shares of £5 each.

Directors.

ANTHONY BANNISTER, ESQ., J.P., late Chairman of the Hull and Holderness Railway Company, (now incorporated with the North Eastern Railway Company,) Kingston Lodge, Hessle.—CHAIRMAN.

JAMES YOUNG, ESQ., of Owthorne, Holderness,—VICE-CHAIRMAN.

WILLIAM BAILEY, ESQ., (of the Firm of Bailey and Leetham, Steam Shipowners, Hull and London,) Director of the Dock Company, at Kingston-upon-Hull, Field-House, Anlaby; and Winestead Hall.

ARTHUR WILSON, ESQ., (of the Firm of Thos. Wilson, Sons & Co., Steam Shipowners, Hull) Kirk Ella.

HORATIO HARRIMAN AYRE, ESQ., The Park, Kingston-upon-Hull, Merchant.

THOMAS HALLER, ESQ., Kingston-upon-Hull.

THOMAS ALBAN Mac MANUS, ESQ., M.R.C.S., L.S.A., Withernsea.

Solicitor.

FREDERIC FEARNLEY AYRE, ESQ., HULL.

Bankers.

MESSRS. SAMUEL SMITH BROTHERS AND COMPANY, HULL.

PROSPECTUS.

OBJECTS OF THE COMPANY.

The objects for which this Company is established are fully detailed in the Memorandum of Association, to which attention is invited. The following are however the principal.

The improvement of the Townships of Owthorne and Withernsea, in Holderness, in the East Riding Yorkshire, by the carrying out of some one or more of the following among other objects.

1.—The purchase and sale of Land in the said Townships.

.—The protection of the Coast from the encroachments of the Sea.

3.—The formation of an Ornamental Promenade.

4.—The erection of a Pier.

5.—The conversion of Agricultural Land into Building Land, laying out Streets, Roads, Drains, &c.

6.—The acquisition by purchase or otherwise of the Queen's Hotel, Withernsea.

7.—The erection of a Spa Saloon, and providing recreation and amusement for Visitors and Residents.

8.—The acquisition by purchase or otherwise of Gas Works, and the supplying of the Villages with Gas.

DESCRIPTION OF WITHERNSEA.

The two adjoining Villages of Owthorne and Withernsea, commonly known under the latter name, are situate on the East Coast of Yorkshire, distant 16 miles from Hull, from which place there is Railway communication.

INCORPORATION OF COMPANY.

The Company was formally incorporated on the 15th day of November, 1870, but no public action was taken until all the land necessary for the profitable carrying on of the Company, was purchased or secured.

PURCHASE OF LAND.

The Directors have contracted for the purchase of about 44 acres of land (coloured pink on the Plan) at very reasonable rates. THE AGRICULTURAL RENTS RETURN BETWEEN 3 AND 4 PER CENT. ON THE PURCHASE MONEY.

They are also negotiating for the purchase of about 150 more acres of land, which they hope to secure on still lower terms.

WORKS OF DEFENCE.

Joint Works of Defence now being carried on by this and the North Eastern Railway Company

The Directors have erected Works of Defence from the Sea for the whole of the land on the Coast purchased by them, upon the same plan as that adopted by the North Eastern Railway Company, under the advice of their Engineer, THOMAS HARRISON, Esq., for the protection of their land, (coloured green on the Plan) and similar to those erected at Spurn by the Board of Trade.

IMPROVEMENT OF WITHERNSEA, and INCREASE OF VALUE OF COMPANY'S PROPERTY.

Projected further Improvement of this Company's Property

The Directors propose immediately to carry out the following works, which will be sources of profit in themselves, and combined, will render Withernsea so attractive a watering place, and so desirable a place of residence for gentlemen engaged in professional and mercantile pursuits in Hull and Neighbouring towns, that the effect must be to create a considerable demand for building land, and to enhance the value of such land accordingly.

WATER AND DRAINAGE.

Effective system of Water and Drainage

This Company will give its immediate attention to the carrying out, in combination with the local authorities, of an abundant supply of pure water, and of a perfect system of drainage.

The prospectus of the Withernsea Pier, Promenade, Gas & General Improvement Company, issued in 1872. Marlinova Collection

the original plan and it is now to be opposite the railway station. Some piles denoting its position have been put down and soundings for the bottom taken during the past week.

The 1872 order was repealed the following month and a new Provisional Order was applied for by the Withernsea Pier and General Improvement Company.

Preparation work for the pier continued apace and on 6 February 1875 the *Withernsea Chronicle* reported:

we are glad to be in a position to state that the preliminary operations in connection with the Withernsea Pier are fast approaching their completion, and the actual building of the pier will commence very shortly. During its formation, we have no doubt that many will avail themselves of a visit to the place to witness its construction.

The building of the pier commenced later that month and the driving in of the first pile was reported in the *Withernsea Chronicle* on 27 February 1875:

WITHERNSEA PIER – the first pile towards the formation of this pier was put in position on Monday last, the operation being performed by Jas. Young Esq (vice-chairman), and H.H. Ayre, Esq. It was not intended to make any public demonstration on the occasion, consequently the ceremony was only attended by few persons other than those connected with the works. A sealed bottle containing a copy of the 'Withernsea Chronicle' and sundry other papers was lowered with the pile, and among them was the record "The Withernsea Pier and General Improvement Company Limited – the first pile of the pier, erected by the above company, was fixed into position on the 22nd February 1875, by James Young, Esq, vice-chairman of the company." The officers of the company are: Anthony Bannister, Esq, JP, Hessle, chairman; James Young, Esq, Owthorne, vice-chairman; William Bailey, Esq, Aulaby; Arthur Wilson, Esq, Kirkella; H.H. Ayre, Esq, Owthorne; Thomas Haller, Esq, Hull; Thomas A. MacManus, Esq M.R.C.S. L.S.A., Withernsea. Solicitors – Ayre, Hodgkinson and Thorpe; secretary, Mr Rymer, Hull; designer and engineer, Mr Robert Pickwell, Hull; consulting engineer, Mr Thomas Cargill, London; contractors, Messrs. J. Oswald Gardiner & Co., London. The pier will be a fine specimen of modern coast engineering, running out a total length of 1,230ft, having a width of 21ft deck, and a length of 18ft above high water at spring tides. At the land end there is to be a brick and stone approach, with seawall, and on either side an ornamental toll house, with central gates. At the sea end the pier is enlarged so as to allow of refreshment and grand saloons. This will measure 100 feet by 60 feet. The structure is to be supported by pairs of cast iron piles which are screwed through the sand to a depth of six or seven feet into solid boulder formation. The piles will form Corinthian columns, eleven inches in diameter, finished with ornamental metal caps; each pier of piles and columns is securely strutted and braced together by strong wrought-iron struts and braces, the clear distance from one pair to the next being 40 feet, which is spanned by two strong wrought-iron lattice girders, securely bolted down to the columns, and well braced horizontally and vertically. On the top of these girders is secured the deck, which is of redwood timber and deals, made to resemble a ship's deck. There will be seats with ornamental standards and backs, running from end to end, on each side of the pier. At intervals, the deck and seats project beyond the main line of the pier, in the form of bays, so as to give a slightly better sea view. Provision is also made for a light tramway under the deck, for loading and discharging fishing and other merchandise (the tramway was not built).

Unfortunately, within a month of the works commencing, the *Withernsea Chronicle* of 20 March 1875 had to report a fatal accident:

SERIOUS ACCIDENT AT WITHERNSEA – A BOY KILLED – in connection with the erection of the pier, at this place, a crane had been constructed to raise the iron piles and girders over the promenade. On Thursday morning at about five minutes to eleven, a girder had been carried and delivered by the crane, when it was being brought back for further work – instantly and without a moment's notice the upright gave way, with the jib, falling with a crash, and in its fall crushing beneath its ponderous weight a poor fisher lad, called William Davidson, aged 17, and killing him on the spot. The accident has produced a deep gloom in the village, and heartrending sorrow to the parents and relatives. Davidson was one of the crew of the lifeboat and the Honorary Secretary of the station has ordered the flag thereat to be half-hoisted until after the funeral.

By May 1875, twelve piles had been driven into the foreshore before the work was ordered to be stopped as the Provisional Order had not been granted. However, the work was soon resumed and in September the order was granted.

The pier met with another mishap in July 1875 when strong north-westerly winds wrecked the staging used by the contractor to secure the piles to the pier. Further storm damage occurred on 26 February 1877 when strong winds and heavy seas washed away two or three piles at the end of the pier.

Nevertheless by this time, the structure was largely complete and on 5 March 1877 Thomas Cargill wrote to the Board of Trade requesting that a section of the pier be allowed to be opened before Easter. Their reply stated:

> In accordance to the Withernsea Pier Order 1875 no rates can be taken for the use of a portion of the pier until the entire pier is completed and when the pier is completed the certificate referred to in section 7 of the order can be applied for.

The last pile was driven in on 9 June 1875, and in celebration the band from the Promenade Gardens proceeded to the end of the pier with dignitaries. The pier was bedecked with flags and Mr Ayre, on behalf of the directors, thanked those present and proposed three cheers for the workmen.

The pier was opened to the public at a cost of a penny per person on 17 August 1875, although without formal ceremony as the toll houses and approaches had still to be completed. An inspection of the landing stage also found it not to be suitable and rebuilding was necessary. A red warning light, sanctioned by Trinity House, was placed at the end of the pier.

The completed pier was a little shorter than originally planned, at 1,196ft rather than 1,230ft, 14ft wide and stood 16ft above high water. Seating was provided along the length of the pier and a small saloon was built on the rectangular pier head. The pier was a traditional cast iron structure with cast iron screw piles of 10in diameter in the neck and 11in in the head, raked inwards and braced transversely by diagonal struts and round iron ties. These piles supported lattice girders by means of wrought iron plates bedded on the tops of the columns; transverse joists carried the wooden decking.

The completed pier entrance boasted an unusual brick-built castellated gateway, supposedly modelled on Conwy Castle. To ensure stability, the foundations of the gateway were embedded in the clay, and to enable maintenance to be carried out without the need for further excavation, Cargill had a tunnel dug beneath it that ran below the pier to an exit door on the beach.

The pier's landing stairs were finally opened on 21 August 1878. They were erected by W Thompson of Withernsea and proved immediately popular with the town's fishermen. However an application for a spirit licence for the saloon was refused on 7 September. Anthony Bannister passed away in July, just as his beloved pier was nearing completion.

A report on the pier's first full season was submitted at a meeting of the Withernsea Pier & Improvement Company in May 1879:

Withernsea Pier just after completion 1878. Marlinova Collection

The general meeting of the company was held in the saloon on the pier last Wednesday, and was attended by a large number of both local and distant shareholders. A cold collation was provided, after which the chair was taken by James Young Esq, the deputy chairman. The balance sheet was presented with the report of the directors, and after a few comments both were passed. The accounts showed that no dividend could be passed this year, but the position of the company was of a sound and substantial character. The pier had been visited by over 60,000 persons during the past year, and was likely to be made still more attractive during the coming season.

On 24 May 1879 the pier refreshment rooms were leased to Messrs Smith & Wood of Hull. The pier's attractions were advertised on 2 June as

New Pier, quarter a mile in length, brass and string bands on pier, free dancing on pier, the 'Bessemer Ship Grand Buffet' on the pier – also in Withernsea Gardens, which has a skating rink.

During July and August the D'Almaine family were that attraction in the pier saloon with their vocal quadrilles and violin concerts. A farewell benefit concert was held for them on Thursday 28 August 1879.

The Directors report for 1879 concluded:

The pier has been well patronised, but owing to the unusual inclemency of the weather during the season, the receipts have not been equal to that of last year.

An artists' view of Withernsea Pier broken in two by the *Saffron* during a storm on 28 October 1880. The wrecked vessel can be seen on the beach. A further ship, *Jabez*, hit the end of the pier and sank with all hands. Courtesy of David Cookson

The 1880 season began with high hopes on Whit Monday:

> Grand opening of the new promenade, pier, gardens and skating rink. Arrangements have been made for dancing in the saloon, and brass bands and strings have been engaged to supply the music. Cheap tickets will be run from Hull. The holiday festivities attracted some 4,000 visitors by rail, and the pier and gardens were well patronised.

The band engaged to play in the pier saloon was led by Mr Mann. They commenced their engagement on Monday, 7 June, performing on the pier in the morning and at the skating rink in the afternoon and evening.

The 1880 season proved to be successful one, but on 28 October disaster struck, when during a fierce storm, two ships hit the pier. The Colchester vessel *Jabez* hit the end of the pier and sank with all hands, whilst the coal barge *Saffron* punched a 180ft hole through the middle of the pier and came to rest on a nearby groyne. Her crew sat out the storm until the next morning and then lowered a rope and walked to safety. The *Saffron* (bound from Southampton to Sunderland) had been one of a fleet of ships which had set out from the shelter of the Humber during a lull in the bad weather to continue their journey northwards. Around eight o'clock, the vessel was near Flamborough Head when suddenly the wind increased to storm force, unleashing the fury of the sea. The captain of the *Saffron* decided to head back for the Humber, but the wind ripped away all the sails, and with torrential rain making visibility impossible, the vessel was left to the mercy of the wind and the sea. She was helplessly driven southwards along the coast until she crashed into the pier around one o'clock.

The drama was described by the captain of the *Saffron*:

The grave of the crew of the *Jabez*, lost when the vessel hit the end of Withernsea Pier on 28 October 1880. Courtesy of Frank Hobson

The vessel got under way leaving the river at high water. All went well till after eight o'clock in the evening, the vessel sailing merrily with a westerly wind. At eight o'clock there was every indication that the voyage would soon terminate prosperously. It was at that time raining fast and the Flamborough Head light was just visible. All at once, at about ten past eight the wind suddenly chapped round to the East North East and the hurricane was upon us. The ship put about to seek the shelter of the Humber, so suddenly and so fearfully did the gale strike the brig, that no efforts could be made to reef the sails or furl them and sail after sail was blown away until the vessel was completely at the mercy of the wind and sea. Helplessly the craft was driven along the coast. Each hour the sea and wind became rougher whilst the rain fell in such torrents that the crew could not see many yards in any direction. About one o'clock in the morning the look out hand forward thought he saw something directly ahead but he could not make out with anything like distinction what it was. All at once Withernsea Pier loomed right across the bows and the resistance this offered caused her to swing round and she drove broadside through the pier.

The damage to the pier was described in the *Withernsea Chronicle* on 13 November 1880:

Withernsea Pier in the 1880s, showing the section rebuilt in wood after the *Saffron* collision of 1880. Courtesy of Jack Whittaker

> The late storm – At low water may be seen the fallen wreck of the pier, the lattice girders, some intact and scarcely damaged by their fall on the soft beach below, some twisted and broken, lie half buried in the sands, some carried or dragged by the drifting vessel 60 yards or more from the spot which they once spanned; the broken and half-embedded columns, the fractured brackets, and twisted tie rods all in one confused mass.

The pier was left un-repaired and on 18 June 1881 the *Withernsea Chronicle* reported:

> The pier (Withernsea), the structure, which in its present condition is a great drawback to the enjoyment of visitors, is undergoing further demolition, and suggests speedy action in its reconstruction. The breach is becoming lamentably wider, and if allowed to exist another winter, the damage will be incalculable. The strong winds last week took another length of the pier, the deck of which had for some time hung down in a threatening manner.

The report seemed to spur the Withernsea Pier & Improvement Company into repairing the pier and by the autumn the gap in the structure had been repaired using wooden supports. However, the cash strapped company was in financial trouble and in December 1881 it was

WITHERNSEA
PIER AND PROMENADE.
NOW OPEN.
Admission : Pier and Promenade, One Penny.

REFRESHMENTS.
LAWN TENNIS, ARCHERY, and BRASSES.

A large Marquee for Hire on very moderate terms, to seat 500, suitable for Pic-nic Parties. School Treats, etc., where all kinds of Games may be carried on during the day.

Apply to Pier Office, D. MURRAY.

Pier Road RESTAURANT,
Dinners and Teas provided.

Comfortable Apartments, with splendid Sea view.

D. MURRAY, *Proprietor.*

An advertisement for Withernsea Pier and Promenade in 1884. Marlinova Collection

recommended that they be wound-up, although they were not finally dissolved until 29 July 1902.

The pier and promenade were leased out to David Murray and 1882 proved to be a modest season. Sadly however, the pier suffered a further calamity on 6 March 1883 when a stormy sea washed away the pier head and its saloon, as described by the *Withernsea Chronicle*:

DESTRUCTION OF THE PIER – we are sorry to inform our readers that this handsome structure was destroyed whilst the gale was at its height on Tuesday. The pier cost the Withernsea Pier and Improvement Company the sum of £14,000 and it was opened to the public in the year of 1878. At the outer end was a spacious saloon and refreshment rooms, and for two summers it proved a great attraction to visitors. Since that time it has been singularly unfortunate. In the great gale of 28th October 1880, a disabled brig, the 'Saffron', of Sunderland, drove completely through the structure, making a gap of about 150ft long. In the following summer the gap thus made was filled in with wooden piles, the rest of the upright work, and in fact everything but the deck, being of iron. For the coming season the directors had still further improved the pier by placing in the saloon the fittings which once graced the very handsome swinging saloon of the Bessember steamer, which was designed to carry passengers from Dover to Calais free of seasickness. The steamer was a failure and her saloon fittings were taken out of her; and ultimately purchased by the Withernsea Pier Company for their saloon, and they had just got the place elaborately fitted. It is said they were advised not to put them in before the winter, and even to remove them again after they had been put in, lest any accident occurred to the pier, but they would not listen to this advice, and now they are clean gone, for whilst the gale was at its height on Tuesday fully half the pier was swallowed. The gale was the worst that has been experienced along the coast during the exceptionally stormy winter. The wind began to grow in violence at an early hour in the morning, the gale being at its height about noon. The wind at the time was slightly to the eastward of north, and the sea as the day wore on began to roll very high, breaking on the beach with a violence most unusual even on this exposed section of the coast. For some miles around the sea was churned into foam, and the sand above the water line was driven in tons over the low cliffs, being deposited in the adjoining fields, in which the ground is covered to a depth of several feet. Towards noon the attention of the inhabitants was called to the outer end of the pier, on which the large saloon stood. The whole structure was seen to be swaying about, and when a higher wave than common rushed in amongst the iron piles it was seen that it shook the pier for several hundred yards. About twelve o'clock with a noise that could be heard above the roaring of the wind and waves, the saloon was seen to topple over bodily to the southward, and one after another the iron piles snapped off, and the deck of the cross portion on which the saloon had stood broke up and was washed away, the sea being strewn with floating planks, the bulk of which, judging by the quantity of wood now strewn along the beach, having been cast on the shore section by section, the remaining portion of the pier, up to where the wooden portion stood, was washed away, the sound of the iron piles being snapped being described by one of the spectators as like the discharge of artillery. More than half the pier, and that the most costly part, has completely disappeared, and there is no doubt the remaining portion is in a very shaky condition. On Wednesday mornings he inhabitants were busy collecting the deck planks and seats of the pier, which had come ashore, but by the time they had been placed in convenient piles on top of the cliff, out of reach of the waves, the police came down upon them and prevented their removal. The bulk of the iron piles and cross girders no doubt lie where they fell, but portions of the ornamental ironwork came ashore with the deck planks and seats miles away from the scene of the disaster. As to the saloon, there was a report on Wednesday afternoon that it had washed ashore near Spurn in a very wrecked condition. One of the spectators states that the sea never once reached the deck of the pier, and the catastrophe was entirely due to the force of the wind, which blew directly on the longest side of the saloon.

The Board of Trade was informed of the wrecked pier by a telegram from the Inspecting Commander at Hull on 12 March:

Withernsea Pier and light gone; with it many iron stumps standing extremely dangerous. Should be repaired at once. A further report seven days later stated: Wreck off Withernsea Pier found to consist of some portion of a pier, not a vessel, it is in track of coasters.

Around half the pier remained, and the Withernsea Chronicle suggested that a T-cross section should be placed on the end to provide a new pier head. On 14 July 1883 the paper reported on the removal of the wrecked section:

During the past few days the remainder of the broken piles, which had been left standing above the low water ever since the destruction of the pier by the storm in March last, have been successfully removed by dynamite charges. The operations connected therewith have been ably carried out under the direction and superintendence of Mr D Murray.

The surviving section of the pier continued to be used, and it appears Murray added a wooden T section onto the end. The pier was opened for the 1884 season on 7 June. Admission to the pier and promenade was a penny.

That same year saw the pier's contractor, J Oswald Gardiner, appearing at the London bankruptcy court. Gardiner claimed that his liabilities of £4,318 were largely due to the cost of litigation against the Withernsea Pier Company, who owed him £1,479. The court recorded that Gardiner

> had entered into a contract with the Withernsea Pier Company to construct a pier and promenade, to purchase gasworks and recreation grounds, and to carry out general improvements at Withernsea for £8,200. When the contract was completed he had received £6,300, and upon the work being surveyed and measured a further sum of £5,459 was held to be due to him. The company failed to pay him, and the result of an action which he had brought resulted in the arbitrator awarding him £1,500 and costs. He had not received 1s of that money and had estimated his losses on that contract at £4,700.

At Whitsun 1885 it was recorded that the pier was crowded with pleasure seekers. Murray continued to run it for the rest of the decade and in 1888 *schoolchildren, orphans and blind people allowed free on the fine marine walk.*

On 15 March 1890 the pier had a narrow escape when *half a ship's keel struck the wooden piles Mr Murray put in 5 or 6 years ago and got jammed between a wooden and iron one.* Unfortunately, this incident was just the prelude to another night of calamitous drama on 20 October 1890 which saw another 300ft of the pier disappear into the waves. The culprit was the Grimsby fishing smack *Genesta*, which had run aground the previous evening at Waxholme with the loss of the captain, Henry Hill. Nevertheless the grounded vessel hadn't suffered too much damage and on the following day it was acquired by a group of local businessmen for £26. They hardly had time to admire their new investment before a further gale prompted the waves to break the vessel up. The *Withernsea Chronicle* continues the story:

> Mr D. Murray became anxious about the pier, and on turning out he noticed that the red light which he has to keep there had been put out by the wind and sea, but it was impossible that he could go out to re-light, because some wreckage of some kind, supposed to be a portion of the 'Genesta', had gone clean through the pier, carrying away the wooden piles, at the inner end of that portion which ten years ago was destroyed by the brig 'Saffron'. The 'Genesta' has broken up; and is strewed all along the beach, and there is sufficient wreckage to also denote the destruction of some other vessel.

With just 300ft of it now remaining, the broken and battered pier was looking a very sorry sight indeed. At the inquest on the *Genesta's* captain, the coroner doubted if the tragedy would have occurred if a guiding light had been located at Withernsea. As a result of his findings, the building of the lighthouse was started in 1891, and on 1 March 1894 it shone out its first beam over the North Sea.

Alas, for poor old Withernsea Pier, the lighthouse had arrived too late. On 22 March 1893 the pier was effectively destroyed when the storm damaged steel vessel *Henry Parr* (formerly *Dido*) crashed into it at high speed, sending a shower of sparks over the many spectators on the promenade who had ventured out on the bright moonlit night to witness the goings on.

All that remained of the pier was a mere 50ft, which survived until 1903 when it was removed during reconstruction work on the sea wall. Two of the cast iron support piles however remained imbedded in the beach for a short time until they too were removed.

The pier lives on however in the castellated gateway, which still survives to this day and has become one of the features of the town, even appearing on its welcoming sign. The two towers of the gateway are usually referred to as the 'Pier Towers' and they have been used for various purposes over the years. Soon after the pier's demolition, the north tower became the Beach Master's office, while the south tower was a penny bazaar and gift shop. Pierrot shows often used the gateway as a backdrop, and in the 1950s the south tower was used as a coastguard station. Today they still provide a convenient rendezvous for holidaymakers and residents alike, who arrange to meet at the 'castle'.

A postcard showing the remaining 50ft of Withernsea Pier; posted in the year the pier was demolished 1903. Marlinova Collection

Withernsea Pier Gates c.1903, with a view of the pier deck just visible on the right. Marlinova Collection

A Valentines postcard issued c.1905 captioned 'Remains of the Pier, Withernsea'. In addition to the pier entrance building, a pair of iron supports can be seen on the beach. Marlinova Collection

The Withernsea Pier Gates form a backdrop to a pierrot show c.1907. Seats were 3d for adults and 1d for children. Marlinova Collection

The old Pier Gates, Withernsea as captioned on this postcard c.1910. The right hand side gate was in use as a bazaar. *Marlinova Collection*

Photographer F Donaldson captures a group of holidaymakers on the Withernsea Pier steps c.1913. Four of the group – Doris Hall, Eileen Lewis, Mabel Geary and Edna Wright – are marked and named on the back of the card. *Marlinova Collection*

A 1975 photograph of the entrance to the old Withernsea Pier. Marlinova Collection

Now an enduring symbol of Withernsea, and featured along with the church and lighthouse on the town's welcoming sign, the pier gates are looking spick and span in this photograph taken in June 2004. Marlinova Collection

Chapter Six

A Pier for the King of Hornsea

Hornsea Pier, 1880–97

F amous for its mere, the largest freshwater lake in Yorkshire, Hornsea is an ancient settlement, mentioned in the Doomsday Book. This is indicated by the 'gate streets' – Westgate, Eastgate and Southgate – plus the Market Place, that emanate around the parish church. It was largely an agricultural settlement with fishing a minor occupation.

For visitors, a chalybeate spring was an attraction from around 1778, and in 1807 there were twenty-three bathing machines available for sea bathing. By 1821 there was a daily coach service to Hull. Nevertheless, in 1831, there were only four lodging houses available to visitors until the Marine Hotel opened in 1837. The hotel boasted warm baths, a billiard room and a refreshment room on the beach. Horse racing took place on the beach during the third week of July. The coach service to Hull was increased to twice daily and in 1840 twenty-eight lodging houses were listed, which had increased to sixty-seven by 1846 as houses were erected for the purpose of letting to wealthy visitors.

The population of the town in 1851 was 953. Two years later, Charlotte Bronte spent *a happy and pleasant week* at Hornsea during the late summer of 1853. That same year saw the beginning of Joseph Armytage Wade's connection with Hornsea. A prominent Hull timber merchant, Wade was to become so dominant in Hornsea's affairs he was nicknamed the 'King of Hornsea'. Wade's business interests in the town included the Hull and Hornsea Railway Company, the Hornsea Brick and Tile Company (who supplied the materials for the houses built in the town), the Hornsea Gas, Light & Coal Company and the Hornsea Pier Company. In addition, he founded a hydraulic engineering works and ran a large farm.

Unsurprisingly, Wade became actively involved in local government; promoting the adoption of the Public Health Act of 1858 and the foundation of the Hornsea Local Board of Health in 1864, for which he was chairman from 1864–73 and 1874–89. However the Hull and Hornsea Railway, which opened on 28 March 1864, was not a financial success and the company still had £50,000 worth of un-issued shares in 1866, the year it was taken over by the North Eastern Railway.

As well as bringing in visitors to the town, the railway also encouraged Hull businessmen to live there, which in turn led to renewed building activity. Wade benefited from this by buying land and then either selling it for development at a profit or developing it himself. On fifty acres of

Joseph Armytage Wade, the 'King of Hornsea', pictured about 1870. Courtesy of Hornsea Museum

land he held bordering the sea; Wade erected the Alexandra Hotel (1867), Wilton Terrace (1868), Alexandra Terrace (1869) and Grosvenor Terrace (1870s). By the 1890s, seventy houses had been erected on Wade's land, and furthermore, William Jackson had developed the Lansdowne Estate on a seventeen acre plot along Cliff Road. By 1891, the population of the town had increased to 2,013.

Following the opening of the railway, Wade turned his attention to providing Hornsea with a pier. On 18 June 1864 the Board of Trade received correspondence from Ebenezer William Hughes and William Bage of 5 Queen Street, Westminster on behalf of a pier company in formation. Wade's Hornsea Pier Company was registered with the Board of Trade on 20 December 1865 with a share capital of £10,000 (2,000 shares of £5 each). The company's object was to construct a '1,000ft promenade pier, refreshment room and a landing place for goods, passengers, fish and cattle'. The registered office was the home of William Bingham Henderson at 59 Market Place, Hornsea.

Unfortunately, only 223 of the shares were initially taken up, 100 of which were held by Wade and 50 by Henderson, and by 2 May 1867 only 243 shares had been issued. There was a distinct lack of enthusiasm in the town for a pier and the Board of Trade order lapsed in 1871. The only work carried out was the sinking of ten piles, which locals dubbed the 'Ten Virgins'. They had been placed to test the strength of the current

Martin du Gillon's plans for a pier, sea wall, aquarium and promenade at Hornsea Burton. Marlinova Collection

PROPOSED PIER, SEA WALL, AQUARIUM, PROMENADE & OTHER IMPROVEMENTS.

along the Holderness coast and were positioned on the beach at the end of New Road. An embankment of wooden hurdles was placed to encourage the formation of sand banks and prevent coastal erosion. However a stormy high tide destroyed both the hurdles and pile driving machine, leaving the piles standing pitifully alone.

An application to the Board of Trade for an extension of time was granted and in 1872 Wade renewed his option to construct a pier of 1,145ft. The plans of Eugenius Birch, engineer to the Hornsea Pier Company and the country's foremost pier engineer, were formally approved on 22 May 1872.

Unfortunately for Wade, Mr Pierre Henri Martin du Gillon, a native of Sheffield, had bought land at Hornsea Burton and with the assistance of engineer Henry Robinson planned to erect a pier and harbour some 700 yards from the proposed site of Wade's pier. However access to du Gillon's pier would have to be over land owned by Wade. The two men met to thrash out an agreement and on 20 August 1875 du Gillon and Robinson believed they had reached an understanding with Wade which would allow du Gillon to build a road across his land from the railway station to the proposed pier.

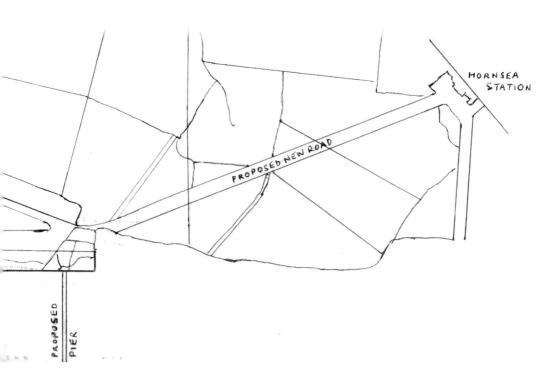

Wade however refused to sign the memorandum of agreement drawn up by du Gillon and failed to keep subsequent appointments. Du Gillon's offer to give up the building of a pier in exchange for the road access to the station was also rebutted by Wade. A series of acrimonious letters passed between them (often through the pages of the *Hornsea Gazette*), leading to du Gillon applying for a compulsory purchase order in November 1875 for access to the land owned by Wade.

In addition to a pier of 1,110ft (to cost no more than £10,000), du Gillon planned a whole new estate at Hornsea Burton, termed the South Cliff Estate. This was to include a tramway from the railway station to the pier, an aquarium, two roads, an 814 yard sea wall and a harbour with warehouses, custom houses, toll houses and hydraulic lifts. A capital of £40,000 was announced and offices were opened in the Public Rooms, Newbeggin. The tramway was to cost £1,800 and would convey first and second class passengers from the railway station to the end of the pier, where various charges would be levied for the landing of goods. The new roads would also levy a toll. Du Gillon dreamt of establishing a whole new town at Hornsea Burton.

Wade, in his capacity as Chairman of the Hornsea Local Board, contended that the land desired from him by du Gillon was earmarked for the town's sewer outfall. In January 1876 the Local Board officially opposed du Gillon's Bill. Wade carried out a series of personal attacks on du Gillon through the *Hornsea Gazette*, claiming *everyone interested would have to take care that the promoter* (du Gillon) *did not get to their blind side. He would have done so with him* (Wade) *if he had closed with his first offer.*

Du Gillon countered with his booklet *An Abridged History of the Hornsea Pier Negotiations – Letters reprinted from the 'Hornsea Gazette' and Preface.* Money from the sale of the booklet was given by du Gillon to the lifeboat fund and on 1 February 1876 the *Hornsea Gazette* claimed that copies had sold out. Du Gillon said of Wade

I did not find it difficult to get on what he elegantly calls his blind side, nothing of the sort, the only difficulty I had to contend with during my wearisome negotiation with him were to find the side on which he is not blind. For the man cannot even see his own interest of that of a community he has so long kept under his tutelage must be stone blind indeed. Why should Mr Wade's hand be against every man who is not ready to do him vassalage as his Lord and King? There is no one who begrudges him his position as 'first fiddle', but why drive the humble band to rebel because he will not allow them to play even penny trumpets.

A Pier for the King of Hornsea

On 28 March 1876 du Gillon's proposed bill, which included compulsory purchase of 19 acres of Wade's land by the railway station, came up before a House of Commons Select Committee. Wade naturally opposed the bill and the compulsory purchase application was refused on the grounds that *the powers, rights, privileges and interests of the Board and ratepayers would be prejudiced by the scheme.*

The decision was met with dismay by du Gillon's many supporters in Hornsea, who blamed Wade for putting personal animosity above the interests of the town. In a letter to the *Hornsea Gazette* du Gillon claimed:

> our DICTATOR (that is Joseph Armytage Wade) has given us another slap in the face, and hopes we will meekly present to him the other cheek – No!

The *Hornsea Gazette* was anti-Wade and lamented the decision in its editorial of 1 April 1876:

> The pier at Hornsea shall not be built. This is the result of the persistent and determined efforts of Mr Wade, in opposition to the Hornsea Pier Bill, which has this week been thrown out by the Committee of the House of Commons.
>
> The necessity of a pier being constructed here has been universally acknowledged ever since the railway to Hull opened, and Mr Wade has been endeavouring for the last seven or eight years to accomplish this object, but without the slightest promises of success. He obtained the requisite powers from the board of Trade, extending over three years, and secured a prolongation of those powers for another similar period, but the time has long since expired, and the powers have lapsed without anything being accomplished.
>
> Our readers are well aware of the efforts made by Mr du Gillon, of the South Cliff Estate, during the last summer, to effect an arrangement between himself and Mr Wade, whereby a pier and sea wall, with an effective defence against the encroachment of the sea, should be constructed. The negotiations broke down, and it became necessary that an application should be made to parliament for compulsory powers to purchase the land required to make the works effective and complete. The land so required belonged to Mr Wade and Mr Potts, both of whom determined to oppose the bill, and unfortunately for the interests of Hornsea they have succeeded in securing its rejection.
>
> The inhabitants of the town, who as it was declared in evidence were almost unanimous in their approval of the scheme, will form their own opinion as to the motives which have actuated Mr Wade in the course he has taken, it being well- known that he has consistently used every means at his command to prevent the scheme being realized; and whatever may be the ultimate consequences ensuing from its defeat, he and he alone will be regarded as responsible for the unfavourable decision of the committee of the bill.

We have always argued that the proposed scheme must have been great advantage to the town, and nothing yet has transpired to affect the convictions on which are arguments were founded. We believe also, and the evidence given before the committee confirms that belief, that no private individual would have benefited so directly and so materially as would Mr Wade himself, so that a satisfactory explanation of his determined course of obstruction is difficult of discovery, especially when we remember that Mr Wade assumes to himself the possession of greater anxiety than anyone else for the development of Hornsea, and claims to have contributed almost exclusively towards that desirable object. However that may have been in the past, in this instance he has inflicted injury upon every ratepayer and property owner, by preventing the introduction of capital into the place, which would have increased the assessable value of the district, and consequently alleviated local burdens. He has, moreover, done that which will more than anything else discourage such enterprises in the future, and render the early development of the town extremely problematical.

Mr Wade has succeeded in his object, and no doubt rejoices over his success; but we do not envy him his triumph. The circumstances in which the town is at present placed call for the manifestation of a spirit the very opposite of that we have now to deplore. Hornsea has just been provided with a costly system of drainage capable of meeting the requirements of a population more than double the present number, and the rates must necessary for some years be exceedingly oppressive, unless something be done to attract an increased number of visitors in the summer season, and induce persons seeking suburban residences to settle amongst us. The advocates of sanitary reform naturally expected that such efforts would be made, and we believe that the force of circumstances will sooner or later compel the adoption of this policy even by those who now decline to assist or so determinately use their power to obstruct.

Du Gillon hadn't given up the fight however, and on 8 July 1876 he registered the Hornsea Pier, Promenade & General Improvement Company (HPP&GI) with a capital of £20,000 (2,000 shares of £10). The object of the company was

the improvement of the Townships and Parishes of Hornsea and Hornsea-with-Burton, in Holderness, in the East Riding of the county of York, by carrying out from time to time, in one or both such townships one or more of the following objections as the Directors may from time to time determine; that is to say, the erection and maintenance of one or more ornamental promenades. The making up of new roads, and the improvement of existing roads. The acquisition, either by purchase or otherwise, of any lands, tenements and hereditaments in the said townships of either of them. The taking of rent, tolls, or other payments for the use of the pier, promenade, or any road, garden, land, or other property of the company. The sale or letting for years or otherwise of any lands; tenements and hereditaments, or any interest therein.

The company was registered at the Public Rooms, Hornsea. The chairman was Martin du Gillon, who held 200 shares. Alfred Maw held 50 and by the autumn of 1876 642 shares had been taken up. Henry Robinson was retained as engineer and proposed a pier 780ft long, 26ft wide with a head of 100ft square; at a cost of £11–12,000. The company's prospectus stated:

> The pier will be constructed to serve as a commodious and ornamental promenade, and will be provided with those facilities or recreation which have made similar piers at other watering places remunerative suitable arrangements will be made and proper appliances provided to land fish. This will supply a long felt want, and afford a considerable source of income. To accommodate this traffic, the pier will be made much wider than generality, affording ample room for a separate roadway, if found necessary, which can be railed off, as at Southport. The pier will also much increase the facilities for boating, which are at present are of a very limited character.

A number of features from the original scheme had been dropped, including the harbour and tramway, whilst the question of land acquisition from Wade to gain access to the station remained in abeyance. The promenade was to be nearly a mile in length with sea defences of nine feet thick. An aquarium remained part of the scheme.

On 20 July 1876 the HPP&GI sought permission to commence works before the application of the Board of Trade order as the 'land had been secured'. The company argued that if the works were delayed until the Provisional Order was confirmed

> the present favourable weather will be lost, and the present price of iron and labour is such that the works can be carried out at a much cheaper rate than will be probably the case when the company would obtain the Provisional Order.

C James Todd, the solicitor for the company accentuated:

> the company is not the same as that which obtained the Hornsea Pier Order of 1866 and 1871, nor is it anyway connected with it, with the exception of ten wooden piles driven into the beach; nothing has been done by the old

company under these orders. It is now more than three years since the last one was driven.

As some assurance that the works will be carried out I may say that the capital already subscribed exceeds upwards of £6,000, all taken in and about Hornsea.

At the first Annual General Meeting of the HPP&GI at the Public Rooms on 8 November 1876 there was *not very much to report on* although an application had been made to the Board of Trade to construct the pier and sea wall. This had spurred Wade's Hornsea Pier Company to apply for the construction of their pier, which was to be 1,200ft in length. On 20 January 1877 the *Hornsea Gazette* reported:

THE HORNSEA PIER SCHEMES – we understand that the two companies have satisfied the Board of Trade's regulations in reference to their application to that body for provisional orders to construct piers at Hornsea and Hornsea Burton respectively. A petition however has been lodged with the Board of Trade against the scheme of The Hornsea Pier, Promenade and General Improvement Company by The Hornsea Pier Company and Mr Wade.

The paper made no secret of where its support lay:

It would be well for the inhabitants to extend their moral support towards the scheme of the Pier, Promenade and General Improvement Company, as it bids fair (subject of course, to the sanction of constituted authority) to be actually carried out.

It seems really absurd, after waiting for years for Mr Wade to utilise the powers he possessed, that we should again be asked to repose trust in an exploded belief, and to reply upon Mr Wade's somewhat illusory scheme, as opposed to that of the Pier, Promenade, and General Improvement Company, and thus forsake the substance for the shadow.

Messrs Wade and du Gillon continued to trade letters in the *Hornsea Gazette*, which on 24 March 1877 printed a map and description of du Gillon's South Cliff Estate at Hornsea Burton:

The pier at the northern extremity of the estate, is the one proposed to be constructed by the Hornsea Pier, Promenade, and General Improvement Company, Limited, the requisite powers for which are being sought in the present session of parliament. It is designated in the Board of Trade's report as 'The Hornsea (South) Pier. The estate comprises about 60 acres (Wade's Hornsea (North) Pier was to be sited 800 yards north of its rival).

In addition to the laying out of the estate, Mr du Gillon has undertaken to enclose and form a public garden or recreation ground; on the principle of the Spa at Scarborough; and also to erect sea defences, of a very substantial character; along the entire frontage of the property. It is intended to apply an area of about 4½ acres, with a frontage to the sea of 400 yards, to the purposes of the public garden; within which, and on the slope of the cliff overlooking the sea, it is intended to erect two blocks of buildings, one to be fitted up as an aquarium, and the other will comprise baths, reading and refreshment rooms. In front of each of the buildings there will be a terrace, covered by a large verandah, and at a higher level than the top of the sea wall, so that in all states of the weather visitors will be enabled to enjoy the sea breeze without any discomfort. The enclosure is to be laid out with walks, and planted with shrubs. A band pavilion, ornamental lodges at the entrance gates, and rustic seats placed beside the walks and in other suitable positions. Flights of stone steps will give access to the sands at convenient intervals. A concrete sea wall will extend along the front of the public gardens, which are to be further protected by timber groynes. A concrete breastwork, with groynes, along the rest of the frontage of the estate will afford complete protection from the sea.

An idea of the extent of the proposed work will be best conveyed by mentioning that the estate as laid out will furnish sites for about 500 houses; of which about 100, viz, those on the esplanade, will be first class residences. Sites are provided for a church, a hotel, and other buildings. Those will be upwards of 2½ miles of roads, mostly 50ft wide, and the whole estate will be efficiently drained. The sea wall will, along its entire length, form an agreeable marine promenade; and walks are to be formed on the side of the cliff, giving access to the esplanade on the top.

Wade objected to the granting of the Hornsea (South) Pier Order 1877 on the grounds *among others* that the dredging in the vicinity of the proposed pier would injure the beach and sea defences belonging to him. On this representation the dredging cause was struck out of the order.

On Wednesday 13 June 1877 the House of Commons Legal Committee confirmed the Provisional Orders for both the North and South piers. The two Hornsea Pier companies had been warned that if there was any opposition to the bills, only one would be passed, otherwise both would go through. Wade and du Gillon, who were both unsure of victory, withdrew their objections.

The pro-du Gillon *Hornsea Gazette* thought the idea of two piers for such a small town was absurd and hoped a compromise could now be reached between the two parties:

The long-pending struggle for the construction of a pier at Hornsea, - or rather, for the authority to construct one, - was terminated on Wednesday, when the House of Commons confirmed the Provisional Orders for both the North and South piers. Whether this decision will be followed by the carrying out of either scheme remains to be seen. In 1866, and again in 1871, similar authority was obtained by Mr Wade without any tangible result, and we must acknowledge that the present position of affairs does not offer to our view any very hopeful prospect of the realization of the professed object of either company. Our readers are well aware that when Mr Wade, on behalf of his company (the Hornsea Pier Company), held the sole right to make this pier, now called the North Pier, he was unable to attract the requisite capital, and although, stimulated by the rivalry of a competing scheme, he has recently succeeded in materially increasing his share list, he has yet a considerable amount to raise, the difficulties in obtaining which will not be diminished by the fact that the opposing company, with a similar proportion of capital in hand, may at any time commence actual operations. Under these circumstances it is just possible that a waiting policy may be adopted by both parties; and if so the labour and expenditure of the late parliamentary proceedings will be altogether fruitless. Why cannot the protracted contention and rivalry be terminated? No local interest is advanced by its continuance. If Mr Wade is really desirous that the North Pier should be made, and will evidence this desire by proceeding with the work, by all means let him do so. Our predilections have all along been in favour of the South Pier, promoted by the Hornsea Pier, Promenade and General Improvement Company; but this company, as its name applies, was formed with other objects than the mere building of a pier, and while we admit that the latter work is essential, we think it by no means improbable that the company may find means of utilizing its capital that would be equally beneficial to the town, and at the same time more profitable to its shareholders than would be the construction of the pier itself.

On 18 August 1877 C E Weddall of Brough commenced work on the sea defences of the South Cliff Estate for the Hornsea Pier, Promenade & General Improvement Company. Four of the eight proposed groynes had been constructed before a gale on Monday, 8 October overturned the steam piling machine used in their construction. The decision was taken to suspend the work until the following spring.

Du Gillon was elected onto both the Local Board and Regatta Committee in 1878, yet his growing influence in Hornsea could not disguise the fact that his grand scheme of the South Cliff Estate was in serious trouble. By August 1878 only 672 shares had been taken up in the HPP&GI and no money was available to fund the construction work, of which very little had been carried out throughout the year. In April

1879 the Hornsea Pier, Promenade & General Improvement Company was declared bankrupt and on 1 May at a meeting at the Public Rooms was formally wound up.

Du Gillon blamed his failure on the cost of litigation against Wade. The defeated man left the area to praise from his fellow directors on his gentlemanly conduct over the past four years.

No work appears to have been carried out on the pier at Hornsea Burton, although the 1879 edition of the *Kelly's Directory*, in error, states:

> The South Cliff Estate, the property of P.H.M. du Gillon Esq, which is admirably adapted for marine residences, has been laid out in building plots to be sold for that purpose and it is the intention of the Hornsea Pier, Promenade & General Improvement Company to build a sea wall in front of it and lay out a part of the estate in subscription gardens with aquarium; a pier is now in the course of erection.

In the meantime, the victorious 'King of Hornsea' had actually commenced work on his pier in August 1878. The Eugenius Birch designed pier was now to be 1,072ft in length and a typical cast iron structure utilising greenheart piles. A small saloon was to be placed on the pier head. The Hornsea Pier Company Superintendent Engineer F.H. Cheesewright supervised the work carried out by the contractors Messrs Bergheim. Work on the approach road and retaining wall had just begun before the Board of Trade ordered it to stop until they had viewed the construction plans. The Board also claimed that the line of the pier going out to sea was also different from that deposited on earlier plans.

The work was resumed but by the summer of 1879 both Birch and Bergheim (the latter owed £2,500) were petitioning for liquidation of the Hornsea Pier Company in order they could be paid. The company had only managed to raise a small capital of £8,700 to build the pier, due, according to Wade, *to the long apathy on the part of the Hornsea people and the severe and vexatious opposition in parliament and the opposition from people outside Hornsea* (presumably Martin du Gillon).

Relations between Wade and Bergheim continued to deteriorate. On 24 February 1880 Wade wrote to the Board of Trade:

> I telephoned you as enclosed this morning in consequence of finding that the contractors for the pier were about to blow up a pile in order to save themselves the expense of taking it out in the proper manner and their so blowing it up would cause additional injuring to be done to the beach and

hasten the progress of the sea towards the lowland at Hornsea and thus cause damage to the extent of some thousands of pounds. I'm very anxious on my own behalf and that of other proprietors as well as in the interest of this village to have such protection as the Board of Trade can afford me. I can understand it can afford the cause, it prohibits the gathering of the gravel or shingle whereby it suppose the beach to be weakened and the operations which the contractors of the pier are carrying forward in an improper manner will produce consequences infinitely worse than can be produced by any gathering of shingle.

I do not confine my complaint to the blowing up of this one pile, but also to the way in which they are dealing with the beach in the whole of their present work.

Wade was perhaps trying to justify why his company had not paid Bergheim. On being asked whether the complaint referred to his pier or du Gillon's, Wade further rubbished the contractor in his reply of 27 February 1880:

In reply to your letter of 25th, I beg to say that the pier is now being constructed at Hornsea is under the Hornsea (North) Pier Order 1877. My complaint is that the contractors, who are doing the work, having broken a pile, with an iron screw shoe to it, in the beach just below the watermark, instead of extracting it in the proper manner by reversing the notion of the screw, are preparing to blow it up and they cannot do this without still further damaging the beach and assisting the encroachment of the sea, it is the more important that they should not be permitted to do this because there is but a narrow crust of slightly elevated land between the sea and a considerable strip of low land and very extensive mischief would be done by the sea if it gained access to this low land. It is crossed by one of the streets of the village of Hornsea and it is so boggy that in the course of time the surface would be torn up by the action of the sea.

I believe the way in which the contractors have already dealt with the beach is calculated to produce mischievous consequences and that these would be very greatly increased by the use of explosives.

On being asked the name of the contractor, Wade gave it as John Simeon Bergheim, 18 Laurence Pountney Hill, Cannon Street EC.

Wade wrote to the Board of Trade again on 5 March, revealing that another contractor had taken over the work:

Sir – I am favoured with your letter of 2nd inst to which I replied by telegraph that John Simeon Bergheim of 18 Laurence Poutney Hill, Cannon Street, London, contracted to construct the Hornsea (North) Pier and that an agent is now there. Mr John Simeon Bergheim has I understand failed (in August last) and he alleges that the contract now belongs to his successor in the business at the same address, namely a Mr Jules de Fontaine. Thus the company dispute and litigation is now pending between them. Nevertheless I presume you would give such notices as you deem needful to Mr de Fontaine as he claims to be in pocession and carrying on the work. A Mr F.H. Cheesewright is on the works at Hornsea, but I believe he is only an agent to Mr de Fontaine.

Bergheim's reply was lodged with the Board of Trade on the following day:

Sir – I have to acknowledge the receipt of your favour of the 4th and to thank you for your courtesy in sending the copies of Mr Wade's letters before dealing with the matter.

It will be a sufficient answer to your question if I tell you that Mr Wade is a timber merchant and is unacquainted with engineering matters and that the pier is being carried out under the immediate valued supervision of one of the best and eminent engineers, the engineer who has had more experience in pier building round the English coast than other engineers, being Mr Eugenius Birch who if you don't know personally you no doubt know by name.

As a matter of information I may tell you that the pile in question is situated 200ft from the low water line and that it is 790ft from the high water line and that the level of the ground at that point is 18 feet 16 inches below high waterline and 3 feet below low water level.

The pile had broken by an endeavour being made to screw it too tightly in the ground. The pile is a timber one 15 inches square and was completely splintered, leaving a stump 14 inches high above the ground. So far from no attempt having been made to remove the pile we have been at work for many weeks trying to withdraw it.

The method that has now been adopted has been to blow up the splinter, kicking the cast iron shoe in the ground.

You will appreciate how little damage has been done to the beach and how delicately the operation has been carried on when I tell you that no less than eight shots of dynamite were applied to the pile itself before a sufficient amount of timber was removed to enable us to put a hollow screw pile over the remaining stump. The charger in each case brought away only small quantities of timber off the 15 inch pile.

That no damage has been done of any kind to the pier you will no doubt be able to find is the case on appealing to the officer in charge to the coastguard station.

Round the pile there are timber piles carrying the superstructure of the pier at distances of ten feet and these have not been in the slightest degree endangered by the dynamite shots that we have tried on the timber stump.

The work at the pile is now complete. A new shoe is left in the ground and a new pile secured in over it.

A gentleman views the wreckage of Hornsea Pier following the *Earl of Derby* collision of 28 October 1880. Courtesy of Hornsea Museum

The *Earl of Derby* lies stranded on the beach at Hornsea after breaking through Hornsea Pier on 28 October 1880. Courtesy of Hornsea Museum

By May 1880 work on the pier was nearing completion but due to the outstanding debt owed to Bergheim the affairs of the pier were placed in the hands of a receiver appointed by the Chancery Court. Bergheim hoped to appoint a manager to open the pier and collect tolls, yet the pier remained closed. On 23 June the contractors held a sale of surplus materials used in the construction of the pier. These included timber, planks, iron and wood blocks, tools, rope, bolts, iron piping, the boat *Polly* and an anchor.

On August Bank Holiday 1880 the Hornsea Regatta Committee used the pier as a vantage point to watch the races. In the following month the pier was finally completed but remained closed to the public. Sadly fate was to decree that the full length of the pier was never to be enjoyed by the people of Hornsea and their visitors for during a terrific storm on 28 October 1880 the 92ft pier head and saloon and 120ft of the remainder of the structure were wrecked when the *Earl of Derby* hit the pier.

The *Earl of Derby* was one of numerous vessels wrecked upon the Holderness coast. She was a 200 ton brig owned by Mr Redway of Exeter and had a crew of eight (including two West Africans) skippered by Robert Foster. She was sailing without cargo from Le Harve to Seaham, County Durham when at around 7.45pm she was caught in a squall of Skipsea. The sails were blown away, and out of control, the stricken vessel headed towards the shore. Distress signals were sent up, which were seen by the coastguard at Hornsea, but shortly afterwards the *Earl of Derby* crashed into the pier. As the mountainous waves rocked the boat against the structure, the tops of the masts fell down onto the pier deck and two girders smashed into the captain's cabin, reducing its contents to matchwood. However the ship's mate and three hands (including the Africans) managed to climb onto the pier and made their way along the deck to safety. The vessel continued to smash into the pier and as the iron supports were snapped off it drove itself through the wreckage before going aground on the beach. Fortunately the five crew members remaining aboard the ship were rescued by a lifeline thrown by the coastguard.

A crewman of the *Earl of Derby* described his ordeal:

> The vessel was driving before the storm on her beam ends. The captain ordered both anchors to be got ready to let go, but with the gale blowing so hard, the order was countermanded and it was deemed best to run in shore, so as to save life. Orders were given to look out for a red and green light, the ship being in broken water became unmanageable. Shortly after Hornsea Pier was seen on the port bow and the man at the wheel put the helm hard-a-port. The vessel did not answer to her helm and the waves dashed her against the pier.

Virtually the whole town had rushed out onto the beach to witness the spectacle. The lifeboat could not be launched as the horses to pull it were unable to face the severe winds and heavy rain, and the lifeboat crew had to stand helplessly by as stricken vessels could be seen floundering amongst the huge waves. The *Hull Packet* described the scene:

> Hundreds hurried from their houses to the beach. The night was pitch dark, but by the aid of a few feeble lights here and there, it could be seen that the waves were running mountains high, whilst the boiling surf was being thrown up to the beach far and wide. The bell of the lifeboat house was rung and the men hurried to their duty but for some time it was impossible to get horses for the purpose of bringing the lifeboat to the scene. Although six powerful horses were obtained and a start was effected, very little progress was made however, the animals being unable to face the wind. Torrents of rain were also falling and the sand was being blown in all directions. The result was that the attempt to get to the boat was given up in despair. If it could have been taken there, it is declared there would have been insuperable difficulties in launching it on account of the huge breakers. Rockets were sent up and in one instance a line was thrown across a vessel but it did not appear to be of much use to those on board. It is stated that a vessel in the offing was burning lights as a signal of distress. These lights suddenly disappeared and it could not be ascertained what became of the ship. Later on, the pier attendant went to put the light at the head of the pier but he could not walk upright. Whilst creeping along, one of his hands suddenly slipped into space and he found that a large portion of the pier had been destroyed.

The crew of the *Earl of Derby* were given food, drink and warm clothes in the porter's room at the railway station and were later attended at the Grosvenor tea and coffee refreshment rooms. The two Africans created a great deal of curiosity as very few people had ever seen non-whites. On the Sunday following the storm the crews of the *Earl of Derby* and *Macbeth* (stranded at Atwick) attended a service at St Nicholas Church to give thanks for their escape. As for the *Earl of Derby* itself, she could not be salvaged and was broken up on the beach with the timber being sold off.

The broken pier was left un-repaired, although some of the wreckage was cleared in December. On 24 December 1880 Trinity House reported:

> The elder brethren are of the opinion that the works in progress will be best marked by two white lights placed vertically not less than six feet apart, and that lights of the same description will suffice for the permanent lighting of the pier when completed.

The correspondence was acknowledged by Eugenius Birch, although on 7 January 1881 the Hornsea Pier Company claimed Birch had ceased to be engineer for the company on 18 September 1879 and had been replaced by R C May of 6 Great George Street, Westminster. The company's dispute with Bergheim rumbled on and it was reported by Wade at the company's Annual General Meeting on Saturday, 26 February 1881 that legal proceedings between them were still ongoing. As a result, there was little chance of the seaward end of the pier being restored and repairs were needed to the 750ft that remained before it could be opened to the public.

On 2 May 1881 the secretary of the Hornsea Pier Company, W J Sawden, was appointed receiver. He was engaged in correspondence with the Board of Trade regarding the buoying of the wrecked sea end of the pier. On 12 May he wrote to the Board:

> The pier has been lighted agreeably with your directions but the lighting of the pier, although at night it may form a warning for vessels to keep sufficiently far off, it does not in the day time warn fishing boats to the small craft which might come close in to shore, not dreaming of any damage under the water at the end of the pier, whereas the ruins stretch out I believe to the extent of about 200ft and as they lie in a confused mass; piles, girders, stays etc it does appear to me that there is some danger which might perhaps be obviated by buoying.
>
> The pier has, I believe not been finished, and as I believe in a legal sense, not in the hands of the company and for my part I have no funds as the pier is not open for traffic.

A buoy was duly obtained and was in place by July 1881. Repairs were carried out to the shortened pier, and on Saturday, 6 August 1881 the *Hornsea Gazette* announced:

> THE PIER – A notice is issued by the Receiver that the public will be admitted daily, from 9 a.m. until dusk (Sundays from 2.30pm) at a penny each. Monthly tickets (adults 2s and children under 12 is 6d each) may be obtained on application at the pier.

Two days later, on Bank Holiday Monday, the pier was reported as being busy.

The pier was closed for the winter but reopened for the 1882 season on Whit Monday. During the Hornsea Regatta on 12 August, the Hornsea Brass Band played on the pier. During the following year's regatta, *the pier afforded a very favourable position for witnessing the sports but was not as well occupied as in previous years.*

Hornsea Pier pictured during the 1880s. The pier was a standard Birch design and similar to the one at Scarborough. Courtesy of Frank Hobson

The entrance building of Hornsea Pier c.1890. This survived the demolition of the pier in 1897 and was used to store fishing tackle until it was removed in the 1930s. Courtesy of Michael Sewell

For the 1885 season the opening of the pier was announced in the *Hornsea Gazette* on 23 May:

> HORNSEA PIER will be OPENED TO THE PUBLIC for the season on WHIT MONDAY. Admission ONE PENNY Day Tickets TWOPENCE special arrangements for schools. PERIODICAL TICKETS as under – family 6s monthly, 3s 6d fortnightly, single 2s monthly, 1s fortnightly. W.J. Sawden Receiver.

The same edition of the newspaper also recorded that the case of Bergheim v Hornsea Pier Company was ongoing. A conclusion was eventually reached, but the pier remained in the hands of the receiver.

Visitor numbers to the pier were small. Apart from offering a bracing marine walk over the sea, there was nothing else to encourage custom. The pier only came alive on the annual regatta days: for the 1886 event 3,500 used the pier, and the attendance remained pretty much the same for the 1887 and 1888 events when the Wilberforce Mission Band provided the musical entertainment. They returned again for the 1889 regatta, which due to inclement weather saw only 2,751 people use the pier. On 3 August 1889, 213 members and helpers of the Hull Blind Institution went onto the pier to enjoy the sea breezes but quickly left due to the cold north wind.

The question of Hornsea's unloved and often deserted pier was raised by a visitor to the town in the *Hornsea Gazette* on 17 May 1890:

> THE PIER, THE PEOPLE, AND THE PENNY. To the Editor of the Hornsea Gazette. Sir – As a visitor I frequently look at the remains of your beautiful pier, and wonder how it is that that which was intended to be the attraction and glory of Hornsea is now so utterly deserted and desolate. Some say the pier itself is not in a fit condition to be open to the public. Some say that the people of the place take no interest in the matter. Others say the penny is the one and only cause of the whole matter. Now, sir, be all this as it may, my object is writing to see what can be done with these three P's, and if by some means their character could be altered and turned into perseverance, pleasure, and prosperity, then my feeble effort would be a success.
>
> As a visitor, I am not supposed to know to whom the pier belongs, or to be acquainted with anything of its past unfortunate history; but looking at it in the light of day, I feel that something could be done so that we as visitors could have the pleasure of taking our families on it at any time, instead of walking on the heavy sands. The latter may be the best for children, but there are those getting into years, and delicate in constitution, who could manage to walk on the pier without any great fatigue. If it is question of pay, I feel

Donkeys on the beach by the pier at Hornsea c.1890. The comparatively busy scene indicates that the photograph may have been taken on a regatta day. Courtesy of Hornsea Museum

perfectly sure there are quite sufficient people in Hornsea ready and willing to pay a small contribution to this object.

I would suggest (to the powers that be) that about twelve gentlemen should be invited to meet and form a committee, and arrange for some plan whereby the three Ps should be turned into perseverance, pleasure and prosperity.

Nevertheless, the pier remained as it was, a bare 750ft of promenade, and for the 1d admission charge, no entertainments except on regatta days. The 1890 regatta attracted an attendance of 3,228 onto the pier, when a 'local band' played, but the number fell to 2,771 the following year when the music was provided by the Waterloo Brass Band. They were replaced by the Railway Servant's Band in 1892 and 1893 and the Cranswick Prize Brass Band in 1894. The attendance figures for these years were not published by the *Hornsea Gazette*, which perhaps indicate that they were not particularly high.

During 1895, the thorny question of the wrecked piles of the lost sea end of the pier raised its head once more. On 22 July Charles Dibden, Secretary of the RNLI, wrote to the Board of Trade:

> Sir Hornsea I am directed by the committee of the Royal National Lifeboat Institution to inform you that reports have been from time to time received from their inspectors of the Eastern District drawing attention to the growing danger to the Institution's lifeboat and crew at Hornsea (Yorkshire) and to the other local boats arising from the remains of the iron piles belonging to Hornsea Pier, which since 1880 has been more a less a wreck. We are informed that the pier company are virtually bankrupt. Continuous pressure has been locally brought to bear on the company to remove the dangerous piles but without results. Some time back a buoy was placed to mark the position of the piles but it has been washed away and lost.
>
> My committee will be greatly obliged to the Board of Trade to whom the foreshore below high water belongs, if they will exert their powers for the removal of the dangerous piles.

The Board of Trade wrote to the Hornsea Pier Company requesting that the dangerous piles be removed. Wade replied on 10 September 1895 that the piles were not easily removed although they would be attended to. In a further letter, on 7 October, he offered the excuse that the ruins could only be got at when the tide was out and the weather was good, and this was not the case at the last tide or on several occasions. Nevertheless some work was carried out and on 23 November the Board of Trade reported that all the dangerous piles had been removed except one. Sawden, the receiver, confirmed on 7 February 1896 that the dangerous

A lone woman strolls along Hornsea Pier, the empty scene showing clearly why the pier never paid its way. Marlinova Collection

piles had been cut off close to the ground and no longer constituted a danger to shipping.

On 3 March 1896, Joseph Armytage Wade, the 'King of Hornsea', passed away aged seventy-eight. A man loved and loathed in equal measure in his close-knit seaside town, the pier had been his big disappointment amongst some notable achievements for his adopted town. From the long struggle to get the structure built, his rivalry with Martin du Gillon and its part demolition almost immediately after it was built, the pier had proved to be one long headache for Wade.

And the pier was not to live much longer than its creator. The winter of 1896–7 saw further attempts to remove the dangerous piles, some of which were washed away in storms, although others remained. Wade's death, coupled with the ongoing problem of the dangerous piles and the pier's inability to make money, led to the winding-up of the Hornsea Pier Company during a meeting at Fowler's Victoria Hotel on 6 February 1897. Nineteen days later, Sawden reported to the Board of Trade that he was putting the pier up for sale, who replied it could only be sold for breaking up. In July the pier was sold for £220 to Edmund Tattersall and John Ellis of Stretford, who were required to remove all the piling.

The pier was opened for its final Hornsea Regatta on 7 August 1897. The entertainment was provided by the Hornsea Town Brass Band, as

An artists' view of the Marine Hotel and the pier, which clearly shows the broken end of the pier. Courtesy of Hornsea Museum

it had been since 1895. The demolition work commenced the following month and on 28 October an auction of the pier's timber was held.

Winter storms however ensured that the contractor's task was not an easy one. A severe storm on 4 December 1897 washed away four of the columns and the contractor's framework. On 15 December it was reported that all of the piling had been removed.

However this proved not to be the case. On 14 November 1898 the coastguard reported that portions of ironwork still remained at low tide and constituted a danger to fishermen. Sawden reported on 28 September 1899 that all the ironwork had been removed; yet many of the greenheart screw piles were left sunk deep into the beach. They were subsequently exposed due to changing beach levels, and some were removed in 1910 and during the 1920s. The old pier entrance buildings survived into the 1930s.

At very low spring tides remains of the pier can still be seen. In November 1996 the fishing coble *Cool Breeze* suffered severe damage supposedly due to the remains of the pier's supports. One of the wooden piles is on show at the Memorial Gardens, along with a section of the pier's seating and the Hornsea Pier Company's commemorative plaque, which was rescued from a scrap timber yard in 1965.

The HORNSEA PIER COMPANY, Limited.

NOTICE IS HEREBY GIVEN that an Extraordinary General Meeting of this Company will be held on Saturday, the 6th day of February, 1897, at a quarter past Three o'clock in the Afternoon, at Mr. Fowler's Victoria Hotel, Hornsea, for the purpose of submitting to the Company, and if it is thought proper passing, the following *extraordinary* resolutions :—

"THAT it has been proved to the satisfaction of the Company that "the Company cannot, by reason of its liabilities, continue its business, and that "it is advisable to wind up the same, and that accordingly the Company be wound "up voluntarily under the provisions in that behalf of the Companies Acts, 1862 "and 1867."

"THAT Mr. WILLIAM JAMES SAWDEN, of Thwaite Villas, Cottingham, "be and he is appointed Liquidator for the purpose of winding up the "affairs of the Company."

DATED this 26th day of January, 1897.

By Order of the Director,

The above meeting was duly held & the extraordinary resolutions unanimously passed & duly registered at Somerset House

Hull 18th Feb 1897.

W. J. SAWDEN,

SECRETARY.

The notice announcing the winding up of the Hornsea Pier Company on 6 February 1897. Marlinova Collection

The old entrance building to Hornsea Pier pictured during the 1920s, when, with the addition of a wooden shed, it was used to store fishing equipment. Marlinova Collection

A wooden pile from Hornsea Pier on display in the Memorial Gardens, April 2001. Marlinova Collection

A length of Hornsea Pier seating situated in the Memorial Gardens, April 2001.
Marlinova Collection

The entrance gates to Hornsea Pier still survive and adorn a house in Beverley.
Courtesy of Michael Sewell

POSTSCRIPT

Saltburn Pier's lone survival on the Yorkshire coast is a testament to the people of Saltburn and their determination to keep the pier as a key feature in their attractive town. The pier's restoration in the 1970s was in the face of a deeply unfashionable time for piers (and the British seaside in general), which saw a number of structures demolished and others closed. The truncation of Saltburn Pier during its restoration made it a more viable structure and has probably ensured its long-term future. The amusement arcade at the front of the pier may be regretted by some, but it is never intrusive to a bracing stroll along the pier deck, and if it helps ensure the pier's survival then it is easily tolerated. Quiet seaside towns such as Saltburn have become eminently more fashionable to visit (and live in) in recent years and the pier, along with the cliff lift, Zetland Hotel, railway station and others, stand as a fine testament to the dreams of Henry Pease.

Nearby Redcar has lost both its piers, proving correct those who forecast that the town could not hope to support two such structures. With the exception of Blackpool, seaside towns of a much larger stature than Redcar have found it difficult to support two piers: look at Brighton (the West Pier), Weston-super-Mare (Birnbeck), Great Yarmouth (Wellington) and Bournemouth (Boscombe Pier). Like many working-class resorts, Redcar had a difficult period during the 1970s and 1980s and would have found it difficult to keep a viable pier going. The loss of the pier pavilion in 1981 was regrettable, but architecturally the pier had long ceased being the wonderfully graceful structure of the Victorian period.

Notwithstanding their awful bad luck, Hornsea and Withernsea piers were never going to be popular enough to ensure a long-term and profitable future, even if they had survived into the twentieth century. However, Withernsea's remaining, and now rather iconic, pier entrance building has ensured that the pier has achieved a measure of posthumous fame.

After 1905, Scarborough was the largest British resort without a pleasure pier. The failure of its 'White Elephant of the North Bay' meant there was little enthusiasm for a replacement. Nevertheless if the pier had been constructed in the more popular and sheltered South Bay, as originally envisaged, it would probably be still gracing the town today.

The history of Yorkshire's seaside piers is ultimately a rather sad story, yet its excitements and dramas also make it a most interesting one.

Notes

1. The stipulation was removed in 1875 to encourage further development following a slump in the Teeside iron trade in the early 1870s.
2. The saloon, although planned, was not actually built.
3. This was a common practice in pier promotion. An engineer and his associates would form a pier company and gain an Act of Parliament for the construction of a pier. They would then hope to transfer their interests to local businessmen whilst remaining as engineers to the company.
4. Designer of Leeds Town Hall and the Grand Hotel, Scarborough

ACKNOWLEDGEMENTS

The author wishes to thank all the following for their kind assistance in the preparation of this book: Linda Sage, Julie Edwards, Daphne Leach, Richard Riding, National Piers Society, Colin Spink at the Scarborough Collectors Centre, Kirkleatham Old Hall Museum, Redcar Library, the late Norman Bainbridge, Anthony Lynn, North Yorkshire County Libraries, Michael Sewell, Hornsea Museum, Jack Whittaker, David Cookson, Frank Hobson, John Whitehead, British Library Newspapers at Colindale, The National Archives at Kew.

BIBLIOGRAPHY AND REFERENCE SOURCES

GENERAL REFERENCES AND SOURCES

Piers of Disaster, Martin Easdown, Hutton Press 1996

Seaside Watering Places, L Upcott Gill, various editions, 1885-1902

The English Seaside Resort: A Social History 1750-1914, John K Walton, St Martins Press, 1983

Seaside Piers, Simon Adamson, Batsford, 1977

Pom-Poms and Ruffles: The Story of Northern Seaside Entertainment, G J Mellor, Dalesman Publishing Company Ltd, 1966

Pavilions on the Sea, Cyril Bainbridge, Robert Hale, 1986

Bradshaw's Bathing Places & Climatic Health Resorts, Kegan Paul Trench Trübner & Co Ltd, 1895

The Guide to British Piers Third Edition, Timothy J Mickleburgh, National Piers Society, 1998

Piers of the Realm, Robin Johnson, Complimentary Studies Thesis, 1976

SCARBOROUGH

The National Archives BT31/636/2672

The National Archives BT31/1192/2648c

The National Archives BT31/4864/32292

The National Archives MT10/33

Scarborough Mercury

Scarborough Pictorial

Times of a Troubled Pier, Martin Easdown, Marlinova, 2005

SALTBURN-BY-THE-SEA

The National Archives BT297/920

The National Archives MT48/39

Saltburn Times

Redcar & Saltburn News

Redcar & Saltburn Gazette

Middlesbrough Evening Gazette

Cleveland Standard

Saltburn-by-the-Sea in old picture postcards, Norman Bainbridge, European Library, 1985

The History of Saltburn, Chris Scott-Wilson (Seaside Books 1983)

The Watering Places of Cleveland, Samuel Gordon, 1869, reprinted by MTD Rigg Publications, 1992

REDCAR AND COATHAM
The National Archives BT31/2221/10488 Coatham Pier Company
The National Archives BT31/30752/3204 Redcar Pier
The National Archives BT31/1573/5152 Coatham Victoria Pier Company
The National Archives MT10/110 Coatham Pier Provisional Order
The National Archives MT10/861 Redcar Pier
Redcar & Saltburn Gazette
Redcar & Saltburn News
Northern Echo
Middlesbrough Evening Gazette
Middlesbrough Exchange
Cleveland Standard
The End of the Pier Book: A Pictorial History of Redcar and Coatham Piers, Peter Sotheran, AA Sotheran Ltd 1981, revised and reprinted, 1996
Redcar in Retrospect, Peter Sotheran, AA Sotheran Ltd, 1975
Redcar: A Pictorial History, Phil Philo, Phillimore, 1993
Redcar in old picture postcards, Peter Sotheran, European Library, 1993
Redcar and Coatham: A History to the end of the World War II, Janet Cockroft, AA Sotheran Ltd, 1985
Come Along Brave Boys, David Phillipson, AA Sotheran Ltd, 1980
Redcar: A Photographic History of Your Town, Maureen Anderson, WH Smith/Francis Frith, 2001
Stand Back Thoo Bits O'Bairns: Stories from the Fishing Families of Redcar and Neighbouring Villages, Hazel Mulgrew, Luftway Publications, n/d
The Battle of the Piers: Resort Rivalry and Pier Provision in Redcar and Coatham 1865-1880, M Huggins, MA thesis, Teesside Poly, 1981
The Watering Places of Cleveland, Samuel Gordon, 1869, reprinted by MTD Rigg Publications, 1992
Picknett Family History: It was a dark and stormy night, HYPERLINK "http://www.picknett.co.uk" www.picknett.co.uk

WITHERNSEA
The National Archives BT31/1575/5160
The National Archives MT10/188
The National Archives MT10/375
The National Archives TI/15827
Withernsea Chronicle
Hull Packet
Withernsea, John Whitehead, Highgate Publications, 1998

Old Withernsea and Surrounding Villages Remembered, Jack Whittaker, Hutton Press 1990

Archive Photographs Series: Withernsea, Mave & Ben Chapman, Chalford Publishing 1996

Withernsea in old picture postcards, Jack Whittaker, European Library, 1985

Seaside Resorts of Humberside, David Cookson, Local History Archives Unit, Humberside College of Higher Education, 1987

HORNSEA

The National Archives BT31/1200/2697cN
The National Archives BT31/2252/10742
The National Archives MT10/7
The National Archives MT10/138
The National Archives MT10/216
The National Archives MT10/224
The National Archives MT10/784
Hornsea Gazette
Hull Packet
Joseph Armytage Wade 1817-1896: The King of Hornsea, Michael Sewell, Hornsea Museum, 1996
The Archive Photographic Series: Hornsea, G L Southwell, Chalford Publishing, 1995
Hornsea in old picture postcards, G L Southwell, European Library, 1993
A Sketch of Hornsea, Jean Hobson, revised edition, Hornsea Museum, 2002
The Contest of the Hornsea Piers, Jean Smith

PROPOSED PIERS

The National Archives BT31/8763/64162 Bridlington Pier & Pavilion Company
The National Archives BT31/1800/6874 Filey Pier Company
The National Archives MT10/402 Filey Pier Company
The National Archives MT10/559 Filey Pier Company

INDEX